Out of the Shadows and Into the Fire

PETER F. LESTER

Published in the United States of America

Brilliant Books Literary
137 Forest Park Lane Thomasville
North Carolina 27360 USA

ISBN:
Paperback: 979-8-88945-297-3
Ebook: 979-8-88945-298-0
Hardback: 979-8-88945-299-7

Character List

Josh Mayer 15-16 Main Character.
Bob Mayer 40 Josh's Dad
Lynn Mayer 38 Josh's Mom
Ed Mayer 17-18 Josh's Brother
Kelly Flynn 15-16 Josh's Girlfriend
Nathan Flynn 11, and Billy Flynn, 9 Kelly's Brothers
Jessica Flynn ~40 Kelly's Mom
John Flynn ~40 Kelly's Dad
Ron Thomas 15-16 Josh's riding buddy
Edie 50+ Waitress at small restaurant north of Beaver Lake
Cal 40-50 Truck Driver who gives Josh a lift to Camp Three Trees
Larry Chang 25 Older experienced cyclist at Beaver Lake Campground
Jose' Serrano 18-19 Employee at Camp Three Trees
Bill Lyndon 30+ Camp Supervisor at Camp Three Trees
Ellie Martin ~32 USFS Supervisor at Three Trees Fire

Prologue

Josh stops on the shoulder of a desolate road on the dry, eastern slopes of California's Sierra Nevada Mountains. He leans against his old bike and squints into the afternoon sun as hot wind gusts rustle the tufts of his blond hair poking out of his bike helmet. He is about 190 miles from home. Not bad for the first few days of his mostly uphill trip with two heavy saddle bags and a sleeping bag strapped to the rack over his back wheel. Fifteen miles or so back, he detoured onto a quiet, if not familiar, side road to get away from the traffic. So far, so good—sort of. The range of his smart-phone is weak. With no online access to check his location, his navigation system amounts to a few road signs, his odometer, and, now, a stop to check his old roadmap.

A sudden gust of wind suddenly rips the map out of his hands. He drops his bike to chase it down. The strong wind, rough terrain, and thick sagebrush are too much. His map is gone. Josh stops running with a frustrated shout at the empty sky, "Damn! What the hell else can go wrong?!"

He will soon find out.

1.

Josh Mayer just finished raking and mowing a neighbor's lawn on a warm Saturday afternoon in early spring. It is a dirty, sweaty job that only pays a few dollars, but he likes the work—just one of several gardening jobs he has around his home town of Argyle.

Argyle is located at the base of the foothills just north of Los Angeles. It is an old neighborhood, reflected in the style of many other wood-frame houses—each with a peaked roof, a brick chimney, shutters, and a large front porch. Tall English walnut trees with their broad, green leaves give wonderful shade for the hottest time of the year. Josh's work includes mowing his customers' lawns once a week, weeding, and, especially in the fall, raking and disposing of what seems like tons of leaves. Some of his tasks at that time of year also include gathering walnuts from the most productive trees and spreading them on raised wire screens for drying.

The solitary work agrees with this quiet teenager wading through what he calls his 'growing-up-time.' Beyond the acne blemishes, the blonde hair that tumbles over his forehead tops a pleasant face which is, more often than not, decorated with a blue-eyed smile. At almost 16, he is a thin 5'8" tall. But he holds out hope for more height and muscle, given the good builds of his father and his older brother.

Josh is a sophomore at Westward High School, where the spring semester is well underway. He likes his classes, although his most recent grades indicate that trying to keep up with both his school work and his after-school and weekend jobs can be a challenge.

The afternoon shadows of the walnut trees lengthen as he collects his tools and heads for home. A few minutes later He walks in the back door and grabs a change of clothes from the laundry on his way to the bathroom to clean up. Stripping down for a shower, he stops to look at his reflection in the mirror over the sink. He winces at the lanky—he'd say 'skinny'—guy looking back at him. Maybe, sometime—hopefully, soon—he'll change for the better.

For a second, he glances at the shelf full of acne treatment products that his mom has laid out for him. He looks into the mirror again and shakes his head at the red blotches on his face, then retreats into the warm shower.

Fifteen minutes later, dressed in a clean T-shirt and a pair of green shorts, he walks into the living room to say "Hi" to his dad sitting in an easy chair and reading the news on his laptop. Bob Mayer puts his computer aside and looks up at his son.

At 47, Bob is a good-looking man, with the blonde hair and blue eyes that Josh has inherited. His build reflects his successful college football experiences as a fullback. At 5'11," he is still in in good shape despite the sedentary management demands of his successful computer sales company. Regular, after-work handball games keep him that way.

Bob started his business from scratch and has grown it wisely to the satisfaction of investors. He demands the highest performance from each of his 55 employees and leads by example. His only compromise over the years has been a pair of reading glasses that he now removes. He looks up at his son. "Josh, we have to talk."

Josh drops into a nearby chair. "Sure, Dad, what's up?"

"I have just been looking at your grade reports. They aren't so good."

Josh quickly realizes that this isn't going to be one of those father-son, "What's going on in your life" discussions. His dad is in his serious mode, drumming his fingers on the arm of the chair, his mouth set in that tight-lipped, all-business look.

Josh takes a deep breath. He knows the signs.

Bob goes on. "You'll be a junior at the end of the term, Josh."

He holds up three fingers, "Your third year of high school. Time is flying. If you want to get anywhere in your life, to be anything, you've work harder now—not later."

Josh isn't prepared for this. He sits up and tries to explain, "But Dad, I …"

Bob sits forward in his chair and interrupts, "Look at what your brother has done! Ed's grades are great. He's on the student council. And you know that's not all! He has found time to be a 'knock-'em-out-of-the-park' baseball player. You've seen his games. To top it off, in the summer, he'll have a job at the city gym! C'mon! He's your brother. Learn from him!"

Josh shakes his head at the thought of learning from his older brother. Taller than his father, Ed is a good-looking, popular high school senior, always busy with his own activities. He barely notices Josh. From their dad's point of view, the age gap between 18-year old Ed and the nearly 16-year-old Josh is only a couple of years or so, but to Josh, it's huge. He and his brother just don't have anything in common.

Josh is upset at his dad's unexpected scolding. He suddenly stands, and looks down at his father. "Dad, I do okay in school. And I have my gardening jobs. In fact, I just finished one this afternoon. And, as far as sports go, I ride my bike regularly on some good day-trips."

He takes a deep breath and pleads with his father, trying to make him understand. "I know my grades can be better. I'm working on them. I'm learning—I'm improving." He is close to tears of frustration as he moves to the doorway.

The tirade doesn't stop. "C'mon Josh, when are you going to realize that your bicycling is not a much of a sport? You have no coaching." He laughs, "And, from what I've seen of your bike, you certainly couldn't win a race! You should be trying out for baseball, track and field—real sports!"

Josh gasps at the criticism of his biking. He loudly defends himself. "Dad, I know about bikes! I have read a lot and I'm a good mechanic. I am saving money for a better road bike. I know where I can get a great used one for only $400."

His Dad explodes, "Listen to me, Joshua! Your biking is for little kids. Get off that damned bike!" Try something else—some team sport."

He stands, pointing at his son. "Why can't you understand? You need discipline! Real sports and coaching will give you that!"

Josh moves closer to the door. He wants this argument to be over.

His dad gives a sharp, frustrated exhale and looks down for a moment. He speaks quietly, "I know you think I'm being tough, but both your Mom and I want the best for you. You're growing up. You aren't a kid, you're a young man now. Regardless of what we want, it's up to you to make the effort. Just do it."

"And while we are talking about your activities, look at you. You are such a loner. You rarely go to dances and, from what I hear from your brother, when you do go, you just stand around!"

Embarrassed to be talking about dancing, Josh knows it is really about girls. He's no match for good-looking Ed.

He tries to explain, "C'mon Dad, Ed is two years older. He's taller, he has a great build and he's good-looking. The girls chase him. I don't dance very well and I'm not nearly as popular. Give me some time. I won't always be this way."

Embarrassment turns to anger as his father's lecture goes on. Josh puts his hands in his pockets and looks down for a few seconds trying to collect himself.

He has had it. He raises his voice, almost yelling, "Dad, why are you always comparing me to Ed? We might be brothers, but we are completely different people! You just don't know who I am!"

Exasperated by Josh's challenge. Ed responds loudly, "Joshua, you listen to me! The only reason you aren't doing as well as your brother is that you are lazy. Your so-called 'jobs' and 'bicycle rides' are more for elementary school students – just excuses for filling time. You're almost 16! You can do much better!"

Josh shakes his head. "Dad, I have to go." His father's angry words are lost in the noise of the door slamming behind him.

A few days later, Josh sits in the kitchen with his mom. His father is attending a Kiwanis meeting downtown and his brother is off to some senior pre-graduation function at school,

At forty years old, Lynn Mayer is a beautiful woman. Her short, black hair frames a pleasant, smiling face that his dad has always said, would 'stop traffic!' Even Josh has noticed that whenever he is out with his mom, many guys are looking.

Brains match her beauty. She teaches part-time at the local elementary school and is active in tutoring gifted students.

Today, at the kitchen table, it is obvious that, even though she speaks more quietly than her husband, she has picked up his message. "Josh, you can do better if you just try harder. Your dad is right. Time is running out. Your third year of high school is just a few months away. You must understand that what you do now will set the pattern for the rest of your life. C'mon, learn from your brother."

Josh is tired of defending himself, only half-listening while she quietly lectures him. He smiles awkwardly when she is through, "Sure Mom, I'm trying. Give me some time."

The spring semester seems to flash by. Josh is as busy as ever with his mix of school and work, just able to grab a bike ride or two on the weekends. One late April evening he sits with his parents at the dinner table. His brother Ed, is at a friend's house working on a last-minute senior project.

For most of the meal, conversation is brief. Josh just wants to finish his meal and get out to the garage to work on his bike. Lynn, glancing worriedly from husband to son, just wants their quarrelsome issues to be settled.

Bob pushes his partially eaten meal away and looks up at his son.

Josh can feel it – another lecture is coming. But this one would be different.

"Josh, you seem to have ignored the conversations we have been having over the last few weeks. I haven't seen any progress with either your grades or with your so-called jobs, nor have I seen any interest in sports beyond your bicycle riding. Something has to give.

"I'm going to give you one more chance to make some changes. If you don't, I am going to wade in with my own scheduling of your activities."

Bob stands and faces Josh with his arms crossed. "The main improvement I'm looking for is bringing your grades up. If you can't show me some progress—some positive changes in the next week—I will insist on a regular study period here at home. I'm warning you, that just might cut into your cycling activities.

"And it's not just grades and sports. I want you to look around for a better job. Get rid of that lawn-mowing work. Learn something. If you apply yourself, maybe you can get a better hourly wage and work fewer hours—more time to study."

He glances at his wife who nods in 'agreement. He looks back at his son, "Mom and I are on the same page on this. We're giving you a chance, Josh, but you must show some effort. Make some real changes. It's up to you. If you are looking for some guidance, look at what your brother's doing. He's a good role model."

Josh feels his temper rising. He has had it with the constant comparisons of his non-accomplishments and Ed's amazing achievements—as if his only goal should be to be like his brother. He stands suddenly and walks out of the room, leaving his meal untouched. He yells back at his father, "Damn it! Damn it! Dad, you just don't understand me! You don't know what I do! You don't know who I am!"

Ed stands abruptly and shouts at Josh, "Don't you dare curse…"

Josh storms out of the house, slamming the door behind him. The rest of his father's words are just noise in the background.

2.

The next day is tense in the Meyer household. Josh and his dad aren't speaking.

His mom scolds her son for his tirade yesterday, "That was shameful behavior! How on earth could you speak to your father like that? He wants what is best for you. Just try to do as he says"

Josh starts to explain, "Mom, I ..." He hesitates, unable to find the right words. He knows he shouldn't have cursed. Still, he feels that he was right. Why did his dad have to be so unfair? Ed can do no wrong, but not so for son number two. "Mom, I have to get to work."

A bright spring sun heats up the afternoon, causing sweat to pour off Josh as he mows another lawn. Halfway through, he stops mowing and leans on the handle of the lawnmower, absently inspecting the neat cut lines he has just made in the green grass. Thinking, maybe his dad is right about his jobs. Maybe they are for younger kids. Maybe there is a better job out there where he can learn something and make a little more money. And, yes, maybe he can study harder, especially that math and science stuff. He shakes his head at the thoughts. He's almost sixteen. Maybe he just has to grow up.

Suddenly, his concentration is broken by a woman's voice, "Are you OK, Josh?"

He looks up to see a middle-aged woman standing at her door. She wears a white apron and holds a broom and a concerned look on her face. His boss.

He smiles and waves. "Oh, sorry Mrs. Burr, no problem here. Just figuring out my schedule. I should be finished in about 20 minutes."

Mrs. Burr smiles as she looked across at the clean garden and the neatly raked and trimmed lawn. "You are doing a great job, Josh! I don't think the place has ever looked better."

Later that week, Josh decides to ride his bike around the town of Argyle to look for other jobs. He stops in front a local plumber's shop. He can see the owner through the shop window, working at his bench, surrounded by appliances and tools. Josh takes a deep breath and steps through the shop door to ask about work possibilities.

John Steeler is a graying 53-year-old, a long-time resident and businessman in Argyle. He has hired many high school students over the years and has a keen eye for good workers. Steeler knows Josh's dad quite well from Kiwanis Club activities.

They shake hands. Steeler asks about Josh's family. As they talk, he is immediately impressed by the teenager's respectful attitude and pleased to see how the boy had grown.

After a few questions, Mr. Steeler says, "Yes, we can use some help here. We have a lot of used appliances and plumbing parts left over from new installations. They are still useful but they need to be cleaned up. I have to warn you, it can be dirty work."

Josh smiles, "I can handle dirt, Mr. Steeler, I've been doing lot of yard work for a couple of years."

Steeler pulls a pad and pencil out of the pocket of his black work apron and writes down a few numbers. He tears out the page and hands it to Josh. It lists the days and hours he would work and his hourly pay rate. "Look this over, and tell me what you think."

Steeler stands with his arms crossed watching Josh look over the figures. "Are you interested?"

Josh is *really* interested! This job could be a huge improvement to his current work. He'd be making way better money than he got for his yard work, and he'd learn some things.

He knows he can't just drop all of his lawn and garden jobs, but he can cut back, passing off a few to some friends. It'll work!

He looks up at Mr. Steeler, "I'll take it! When do I start?"

Steeler is impressed by this thoughtful and enthusiastic kid. After a little more discussion, they agree that Josh can start the job in two days.

Steeler adds, "Josh, in a few months, there'll be a scheduling change that I want you to know about up front. My son will be home from college for the summer. He'll take over your job plus a couple of others at my shop to be full time from June eighth through mid-August. I won't need you then, but if I like your work between now and the time he starts, I'll be happy to have you back next fall."

Josh rides slowly away from Steeler's shop. In contrast to his bike speed, his mind seems to be going a hundred miles an hour. He reviews his new job situation. He can work almost two months for Mr. Steeler this spring. He can save a lot of money. Maybe even buy a better bike! He can handle the summer off. The grass will be growing by then and he'll have plenty of lawn jobs. Perfect!

Josh is a happy guy, pulling a couple of wheelies on his old bike to celebrate. His antics startle an old woman pulling a shopping cart when he passes her talking loudly to himself, "I am improving! Dad will have to like that!"

That evening, Josh manages to be at the dinner table with the rest of the family. He's anxious to share his excitement about his new job. But when his news comes tumbling out, his father's reaction isn't at all what Josh expects.

Bob Mayer pauses in mid-bite and squints at Josh. "Sorting used plumbing parts? What the heck kind of job is that?"

Ed leans back his chair back and smiles down at his Josh. "C'mon Dad, my little brother doesn't know the ways of business like we do. He thinks that any job is a 'good' job."

Ed snickers louder, "Ya know, maybe he's right! He could get an even better job at school – cleaning toilets!"

Bob smiles at the suggestion then advises his oldest son to "Back off, Ed, you aren't helping matters."

Josh is surprised to find himself defending what he thought was obviously a good job. Ignoring his smart aleck brother, he tries to control his temper and explains to his dad. "I'll be making a lot more money at Mr. Steeler's shop than I make for mowing lawns. And I'll learn something about the plumbing business. You said that I should look for something better, Dad. This is better!"

His father still sounds skeptical. "I suppose it is a start – we'll have to see."

Disappointment is apparent on Josh's face. His mom shakes her finger at the words of her husband and older son, "You guys are terrible. Give him a chance! Josh, this sounds like a good thing. Let's see how it develops."

In the next week, Josh cuts back on his lawn jobs, passing some of them off to other buddies but still keeping a few with his oldest customers.

A few days later, he walks into the house hot and thirsty after a long, not-so-good day at school and an afternoon of hard work hauling pipes and fittings around Steeler's plumbing shop. Earlier in the day, he had been late for a math class and a test had not gone well. There is a mountain of homework in his backpack. He steps into the kitchen where Ed greets him with a brotherly punch to the shoulder, "Hey sweaty little brother, I see you have been out doing those 'heavy thinking' jobs."

Fresh from a shower and dressed neatly, Ed is about to drive off to some school function. He laughs as he continues to kid Josh. "I hear that your brainy lawn-mowing efforts are now being replaced by a new, really challenging job. What is it? Something about used plumbing parts? You will have to tell me about that high-tech work sometime."

Josh reacts tiredly, "You know, Ed, if you bothered to get a real job, you might understand the difference between 'work sweat' and 'play sweat.'

Ed responds with a snicker, "Whoa, testy little brother, is your brain-heavy work sapping your sense of humor?"

Bob Mayer walks into the room just as Josh explodes, pointing at his brother and shouting angrily, "You shithead, you wouldn't know hard work if it bit you. All you do is fart around and play all day, patting yourself on the back. Listen to me, you are not as good as you think you are!"

Bob steps between his two sons. "Hey you guys, knock it off! And watch your language, Josh. Ratchet down the temper tantrums. Your older brother can give you some hints about behaving. Why don't you go outside and cool off?"

Josh wants to explain, but he knows it would be a useless exercise. He turns and leaves the room with a quiet, "Sure, Dad."

A minute later, he walks into the workshop behind the garage. Still mad, he angrily kicks over his tool box, scattering the contents across the floor. He shakes his fist at the wall and shouts, "They can't see my side of anything! I'm the little brother so I know nothing! I can't do anything right! Shit! Shit!"

Standing in the middle of the workshop with his hands over his face, he feels a couple of tears. He rubs his eyes and shakes his head, trying to clear his mind of the bad stuff. He looks over at his bike leaning against the wall, takes a deep breath, and begins to calm down. He laughs at himself with a loud, "C'mon Joshua, grow up!" and begins to pick up the tools he kicked across the floor.

Josh enjoys many sports. He attends the games of his high school football, baseball, and basketball teams and watches college and pro games on TV. However, his most serious sport interest is cycling. He got his first bike when he was nine and has been riding ever since.

Bicycles have changed a lot since his first one. Now he owns a road bike. He knows the links to cycling repair sites on the web and keeps a pile of cycling books and maintenance manuals under his bed. A good mechanic, he has gotten his bike in better shape than when he bought it a year ago.

One his favorite times of year is during that great bike race, The Tour d' France. Cycling posters from that competition and several national races decorate the walls of his bedroom.

Josh and three or four of his buddies regularly rode 20 miles or so on Sunday afternoons until a few months ago. Things have changed. With the exception of his friend, Ron Thomas, most of those friends have given up biking for other activities. Josh and Ron now ride on both Saturday and Sunday whenever they can. It is paying off. They are stronger and they have pushed some of their trips now out to more than 30 miles. These improvements suggest to Josh that he and his buddy should start thinking about a longer trip—something for the next summer.

3.

Josh continues to stay away from of his family as much as possible over the next several days. Actually, it isn't so difficult to avoid them. With classes and homework, his lawn work, and now his job with Mr. Steeler, he rarely participates in family meals. "Too busy" is his excuse. He still does his weekend bike rides whenever he can and he is saving some money to buy a smart-phone for some longer rides.

On a bright Sunday afternoon, he is working in the garage of his cycling buddy, Ron Thomas. They have just returned from a more than three-hour trip and are checking out their bikes. It was a good ride, mostly over quiet side roads in the foothills north of Argyle, away from the heavy traffic feeding the freeways that lace across the L.A. Basin to the south.

Ron, like Josh, is just finishing his sophomore year at Westward High. The two cyclists always have a lot to talk about. They have similar personalities and have been friends since elementary school. But they are a contrast, physically. Where Josh is a slender, blond, 5'8"; Ron is a pudgy, dark-haired, 5'5." Height and weight are not a hinder to Ron's cycling ability. His thick legs are powerful and he can hold his own when he and Josh challenge each other in short, friendly competitions on steep climbs and short sprints.

Their older bikes are the heavier metal types as opposed to the fantastically light and expensive, carbon-fiber versions they can only dream about. One of these days, when they can afford it, they will move up in the quality of their cycling equipment. However, for the present, their attention is on keeping the equipment they have in the good shape. Today, their cycling gear and a large collection of parts and tools are spread across the floor of Ron's garage.

Pausing as he works on a brake cable, Josh looks up and asked, "Ron, do you ever have run-ins with your older brother?"

Ron gives a frustrated head shake as he continues to adjust his bike gears, "All the time. As far as he is concerned, he knows everything and I know nothing."

Josh smiles knowingly, "I know how that works! How do you handle it?"

"Most of the time, I yell at him to stick it up his ass—unless my parents are around—then I whisper to him to stick it up his ass."

Josh looks up from a cable adjustment he is working on and exclaims, "That's my situation! My brother thinks he knows all and can do all. Whenever I try to explain to him why he is wrong about something, he never listens. It's like he's a clone of my dad!"

Ron replied, "I agree. It's the *older brother disease*. They think they are our parents but they are really just full of shit!"

Ron and Josh have a good laugh, agreeing that older brothers were a pain.

They tinker with their bikes for another quarter hour—adjusting, testing, and adjusting again. Josh gives a sigh of relief, "Well, bike buddy, I think we're done for the day. These machines should fly the next time we ride them. And, speaking of riding, I have an idea."

He looks over at his friend and speaks tentatively, "I've been kicking around a plan for a bike trip for next June—something much longer than our usual day trips. It would be a good chance to get away from our know-it-all brothers for a while. Whad'ya think?"

Josh's proposal isn't just something off the top of his head. It is the result of some sleepless nights. And it has a double edge as far as he is concerned. Yes, he wants to make a long ride as a great summer adventure, but his idea is also a reaction to his dad's lack of understanding of how important his biking is. He has to get away from his brother's and his parent's unending putdowns about his work and their demands for him to be better at school, despite the progress he knows he is making. He wants to show them that biking is a tough and challenging sport and that he can do it.

Ron stops working on his bike and looks up, wrinkling his brow as he pauses to consider Josh's idea for a long trip. A wide grin breaks out on his round face. "Wow! Josh! What a great idea! Riding and camping—I'm all for it!"

Ron continues to absorb the idea, swinging a greasy rag in his excitement. "You're right, we've been riding in the local area for so long that I think I can get on my bike, close my eyes, and still get to wherever and back. Boring! No maps necessary. Yeah, it's time we do something way different!"

Josh rubs his hands together, "OK, let's get organized. First, we have to do a major sales job on our parents. I think if I tell my Mom and Dad that two of us are going, they will OK the trip."

Ron agrees, "And mine, too. I'll have delay starting my summer job for a while so I better have a good plan when I drop this idea in their laps. We have to convince them that we know what we're doing. And speaking about knowing what we're doing, we better get busy checking out our bikes and organizing our gear."

Ron walks around in a circle in the middle of the garage—thinking—already into serious planning. He stops and looks up at Josh. The questions pour out. "When will we leave? Where will we go? How long will we be gone? Any ideas?"

Josh was ready for these questions. "How about this? We leave just after classes are out and go for two weeks or so. I figure that with the loads we'll be carrying—you know, water, tools, camping gear—we can cover 40 miles a day. We have been doing half of that easily on our weekend rides. We can push our preparation a bit by riding more around here in the next few weeks, to get into better shape. I figure that if we up those rides to four or five days a week, we should be able to do somewhere around five or six hundred miles for our whole trip. Maybe more. Now there is a bike trip!"

Ron is excited about Josh's suggestion. "five or six hundred miles! Yowie! That would be fantastic! Where? The coast? The mountains?"

Josh pauses as he puts his tools away. "I have only just started thinking about that. From what I know, the coast would be nice, except for a couple of things. First, there are some steady head-winds there in the summer, especially in the afternoons going north. Add a few hills and that would make it a really tough ride. And then there is what I think is the biggest problem – heavy traffic. That is a popular route for big trucks and tourists.

Josh takes a map of California out of his pocket and unfolds it on the work bench. He points to the large range of mountains that parallel the east side of the state – the Sierra Nevada. "I'm leaning towards the mountains. After we push over the mountains north of us, we can ride along the east side of the Sierra Nevada range.

"We'll have some climbing to do, but there are some quiet roads up there—lots of room for bikes. From what I've read, the winds are OK most of the time except for a thunderstorm now and then. We can handle that. Above three or four thousand feet where we can take advantage of cooler temperatures and the shade of the tall pine trees. There are lots of public camps near lakes and streams. What d'ya you think?"

Ron is impressed with Josh's planning. He slaps his buddy on his back. "Wow. Josh! You've really done some research! I like your plan for the mountains. You're right, we'll have some tough climbs but I can do without the headwinds on the coast." He laughs, "At least, in the mountains, a good climb is followed by a great down-hill! Email me the links to the websites you've looked at and I'll get myself up to speed on the territory."

The two cyclists talked a bit more about possible routes, then Josh proposes a plan. "In the next couple of days, let's each print some maps off the web and study the area. When we get together for our Sunday bike ride, we can decide exactly which way we'll go. OK?"

Ron slapped his hands together, "This is great Josh! I'm already good to go!"

Finished with maintenance, they both pick up their bikes and the rest of their tools. Ron pushes the garage door open to the busy neighborhood and entertains some passing pedestrians with a funny dance and an off-key tune: "Yippee! Big ride coming up – I'm ready, ready, READY!"

Josh smiles and shakes his head at the antics of his slightly crazy biking buddy. Yes, this is going to be a great trip. He gives Ron a high five, jumps on his bike and heads for home, picking up on Ron's shouts as he goes, "Hot damn! I'm ready to pedal – way down the road!"

4.

Kelly Flynn, a slender 15-year-old, is the oldest of the three Flynn children. Her brothers, Nathan, 11 and Billy, 9, are still in elementary school and she is a sophomore at Westward High.

Kelly wears her Irish heritage well with red hair, blue eyes, and freckled, very fair skin. A little shy, she has some issues with her appearance. At 5'5," she barely has a shape and her lovely blue eyes are hidden behind glasses. And then, there are those braces.

Kelly and her Mom have many conversations about Kelly's concerns about her appearance. Many of Kelly's friends have already crossed the threshold to young womanhood and she feels that she is being left behind. "What's wrong with me, Mom? They are all filling out to be young women—wearing bras. With this shape, I might as well be in elementary school, playing tether ball."

Jessica Flynn smiles at her daughter's dilemma. "Kelly, you know better than that! We have had a lot of conversations about puberty and you know the answers. Some wonderful changes are already beginning. Don't worry. It will happen. I've told you, I was a skinny, pimply-faced sophomore when I was in high school. And I think I turned out OK."

Jessica is a beautiful woman by any measure and, yes, Kelly's talks with her mom—discussions in class—everything promised that "it" will happen soon are awful. Jessica continually reassures her daughter, "The beauty is there; you just have to be patient to blossom into a young woman. It will happen."

Kelly wasn't sure. Waiting is difficult. sometimes she doubts that she will ever see any "blossoming," whatever that is.

It isn't that Kelly doesn't understand the process. She's an excellent student with a talent for math and science—especially biology. In fact, if someone asked her, "What do you want to be?" She'd say "A doctor, an M.D. like my mom."

Her dad, a math teacher at a local grade school, gently reinforces his wife's words, "Not to worry, Kelly. Good things will happen, you'll see."

When her friends wonder out loud about her minimal social life, Kelly tells them that her studies and babysitting jobs that are the reasons that dating is not yet been on her schedule. Deep down though, she knows it is more than that, it's her appearance. Her social disappointments contrast sharply with her academic successes. She is never invited to parties or dances.

Yesterday at school, she reached a low point when she overheard a couple of her classmates – guys – laughing about her in the hallway. Their conversation was about the "…metal-mouthed monster sitting by the window." One was saying, "She looks like a skinny version of some space alien! Especially In the morning, when her braces and glasses reflect the sun. With that red hair flying, she is scary!"

Their cruel words are quickly lost in the chatter of students filling the hallways between classes. Kelly ducks into the girl's restroom to hide her tears of embarrassment.

In bed that night, more tears trickle down her cheeks as she recalls the day's major humiliation. She finally speaks to herself out loud, "Those two guys are stupid and couldn't get a date if they wanted to! It's not important!" Slapping her pillow, she finally cries herself to sleep.

5.

The next morning, crowds of noisy Westward High students rushing between classes are greeted by a beautiful spring day. Kelly doesn't see the beauty. She walks quickly toward the library with her books, tablet, and purse held tightly in her arms. She doesn't want to make eye-contact with anyone, afraid she'd run into the nasty classmates from the day before. That incident was so hurtful and embarrassing.

She passes a giggling group of girls. Juniors. She can't help but notice how teach one had it all—the shape, the hair, the smile – even the walk. She is embarrassed by her skinny body draped in a simple green blouse a pair of Levis and sandals, a drab computer bag over her shoulder. Would she ever be like them? This is another one of those times when she doubts it.

Tears were filling her downcast eyes on her way to the library. She looked up just in time to avoid a bumping into a slim, blonde fellow at the entrance to the library. He did a funny pirouette to step out of her way but manages to drop one of his books at her feet. They both bend down to pick it up, lightly bumping heads. Both speak at once, apologizing, then giggling over their harmless collision.

Face-to-face with Kelly, Josh apologizes again. "Sorry about that. You sure you're OK?"

She pushes her wire rim glasses up on her nose and smiles, "No problem.

"Hey! I think I know you. Aren't you in Mr. Larson's geometry class?"

"Yep I am. I'm Josh Mayer."

One of the first things Josh notices about Kelly is that she isn't wearing any of the makeup that most of her classmates were experimenting with. With her bright red hair and beautiful blue eyes that her glasses couldn't hide, makeup wasn't needed.

She puts her hand on his arm, apologizing again for her part of the collision.

Her unexpected touch disarms Josh. Too often in the past, just a hint of female attention has terminated his ability to communicate. Smiling, he awkwardly runs his hand through his hair, not sure what else to say.

They stand looking shyly at each other for a few seconds. Then, she excuses herself, smiling back at Josh, "I have to get to the library. See you in class!"

"Nice to meet you, Kelly."

"Josh."

Their chance meeting has immediate effects on both of them.

For Kelly, it pushes her concerns about braces and glasses and skinniness and yesterday's experience with her rude classmates out of her thoughts. Josh is there now.

Josh's reaction is a more complicated. With school, jobs and biking, he had convinced himself that he was too busy to try to date girls. Oh, he knows a few and he has attended some school dances. But those occasions usually found him standing alone on the edge of the dance floor, tapping his foot. It didn't help that he felt a bit awkward around girls. Today, though, his encounter with this red-headed girl was different. He can't quite put it into words, but there is the distinct feeling that his old concerns have disappeared.

6.

In contrast to the wonderful spring warmth, Josh's relations with his family have been, at best, cool. Conversations around the dinner table had deteriorated into mostly silence punctuated by a few automatic exchanges. He was glad when his after-school and weekend jobs kept him out of the house.

On a day in late May, Josh turns 16. He hadn't really been thinking about it when he got up that morning until he walks into the kitchen where his mom and dad and his brother, already sitting at the table, break out into a hearty rendition of "Happy Birthday."

His face is red with happy embarrassment. "Wow! Thanks, I didn't think anyone would remember." He looks down for a second, shaking his head, and then laughing. "In fact, I almost forgot myself!"

A small birthday cake covered with 16 candles follow the usual breakfast routine of cereal and fruit.

Immediately after breakfast, Ed stands to leave. He reaches over and pats Josh on the shoulder. "Hey little brother, now that you are a big one-six, you can actually get a driver's license and take out those girlfriends I never see you with."

He laughs at his joke, and stands to leave, "Sorry to cut your celebration so short, but I have to go. You know how it is with us seniors. Big build-up to graduation. Hang in there, my pint-size brother!"

He gives Josh a slap on the back as he walks out of the room and opens the front door. Jingling his car keys, he shouts over his shoulder, "Yeah little guy, with a little more luck, I think you'll make it!"

Josh's dad laughs at Ed's words as he watches his older son leave, "Now, there is guy who is going to be something!"

Josh tries to ignore his brother's not-so-veiled put-downs and what he feels is just one more of his dad's unfair comparisons of his two sons.

He turns his attention to a large white envelope and a couple of presents. The envelope contained a plain sheet of white typing paper. Drawn sloppily in a black marking pen, a stick figure on a tricycle stood over the words, 'Hey little brother, keep on pedaling that tricycle – oops, I mean bicycle. Happy Birthday from Ed.'

Forcing a smile at his brother's lame excuse for a birthday card and crappy joke, Josh picks up a couple of other gifts with more appropriate birthday wrapping plus a card from his parents. Opening one, a new shirt brings a smile to his face.

The second package is a small one. Unwrapping it, he finds a new smart-phone with a note in his dad's writing. 'If you are going to ride your bike to the back and beyond, you better stay in touch with us! Love, Mom and Dad.'

Josh is pleased. He had just about given up on the old flip-top phone he inherited from his father. "Wow! Thanks! I really, really appreciate this!" Then he relaxed and laughed, "Sure, Dad, I'll call you!"

7.

The last two weeks of class are hectic. Josh still has a few projects to finish by semester's end. He hurries to his computer lab, scanning a homework assignment he had just gotten back in his previous class. Suddenly he looks up to find Kelly standing in front of him. Kelly, awash in curls of shiny red hair, her hand self-consciously covering her braces-filled smile, catching Josh in the steady gaze of her beautiful, laughing blue eyes.

They had seen each other many times after their first meeting. In class, in the hallway, in the lunch hall – it seemed everywhere. Sometimes Josh wondered if there was some kind of magnetic attraction between them, so often did they end up in the same space.

He slowly passes her, walking backwards to keep her in sight "Hey Kelly!"

Wide-eyed and smiling, she stops in the busy hallway to catch what he was saying. "Hi Josh! Where are you rushing to?"

"My computer lab. Last quiz before the final today. I have to get going, I'm almost late. Say, why don't we meet when classes are over?"

Kelly calls after him, "Sure! 3:15? Where?"

Josh waves with a big grin, "Our tree! See you there!"

That afternoon, they stood under the light green, spring leaves of a peach tree in an old grove on the edge of the campus. A few weeks ago, they had run into each other walking past this spot and had decided that this would become their special meeting place, a bit away from the craziness of their classmates. To them, it was 'Our Tree.'

Leaning against the trunk, Kelly asks Josh about his computer lab quiz. He is distracted for a moment by the way the afternoon sun highlights her hair. "Oh, I … I … I think I did OK. I'm starting to get it. Those problems you helped me with in the library yesterday really helped a lot. Thanks!

"How is your day going?"

"Mostly good, especially Mr. Burton's class. History. I like math and science, but history is always interesting, too."

Kelly and Josh discuss family and the weather and anything else that will keep them talking with each other. Laughter about teachers and classmates and themselves comes easily. Other times they just stand quietly under their tree with its leaves shining in the sun or talk about the sky and the funny shapes of fluffy clouds that appear and disappear as they drift by. For a shy second or two before walking back to class, they look into each other's eyes.

8.

Despite the brief, fairly relaxed encounter with his parents on his birthday, Josh soon realizes that that his exchanges with them are still not very good. His dad quickly gets back on his case about grades and his cycling and plays his older son's "bigger, smarter, and more successful" card in Josh's face. Josh begins skipping meals with the family, with the excuse that he is busy with school and working. The real reason, of course, is he wants to avoid any of his Dad's nasty outbursts.

Wednesday afternoon Josh steps into the kitchen for a snack before he retreats into his room to prep for a couple of exams. His mom stands at the kitchen sink. "Oh Hi, Mom. I thought that you were out. I'm just going to grab a sandwich before diving into my math and history for some of tomorrow's quizzes." He reaches into a cupboard to retrieve a loaf a bread and jars of peanut butter and strawberry jam. He laughed, "You know how it is, Mom, I need food to study!"

Lynn looks up from the fresh vegetables she is rinsing. "Good to see you for a change, Joshua. You've missed a lot of family meals lately. With your brother wrapped up in all of his senior year activities, he is gone a lot, too. Your dad and I have been having some quiet suppers."

She walks up behind Josh and puts her hand on his shoulder. "We know what your brother is doing, but we are worried about you. We miss you. And it's not just at the dinner table. You have become so quiet lately. What's up?"

Josh makes his sandwich and pours a glass of milk. "Oh Mom, I … er … like I said, school has been crazy lately with final exams coming up. I'm trying to stay on top of my lawn jobs and now there is my work for Mr. Steeler. Just a lot going on. Busy, busy!"

His mom frowns. "I think you might be TOO busy, Josh. Your father and I always enjoy those regular dinner table updates from you and your brother. But now we hardly see you.

"And don't forget that Ed will be graduating in June and by the end of the summer, he'll be away at college. You don't have much time to see him between now and then."

Josh doesn't want to have this conversation. It seems that his parents only criticize him and praise his brother. The last thing he wants to do is to talk to Ed.

"Sure, Mom. I hafta go now. Stuff to do. I'll try to be on time for dinner."

∗∗∗

The next Saturday, Josh is working on his bike in the garage—getting it ready for one more ride before he and Ron leave on their summer trip. His dad walks in. Josh leans the bicycle against the wall next to his tool box and turns to his father. "Hi Dad, I want to talk to you about something. Got a minute?"

Bob Mayer gives his son a confused smile, "I thought you weren't talking to me."

Josh says, "We need to talk, Dad. I know that you have some doubts about my biking activities."

His dad interrupts, "Josh, where is this going? I have heard most of your 'biking-is-good' arguments before. You know how I feel about that excuse for an organized sport."

Josh gives a frustrated glance at the ceiling, shaking his head at his Dad's comments. He raises his voice, "Dad, give me a break. I have thought about these things a lot because you asked me to. Give me a chance to explain!"

Crossing his arms, Bob takes a deep breath and leans against the garage wall. He looks at Josh with a half-smile, "OK son, I agree, I did ask. Go ahead, you have my attention."

Josh had rehearsed his words many times. "You have said that it's important for me to improve my grades. Well, in the last month, my test scores have been getting better. I am studying with another student who is particularly good in math and science. She has been helping a lot.

"And about my job situation. I am still doing yard work, but I am farming out some of those jobs because I am working regularly for Mr. Steeler. I know it's not your first choice for a better job for me, but it is a better-paying job and I am learning something about plumbing and appliance repairs."

Bob doesn't necessarily agree with everything Josh says, but he finds himself impressed with his son's arguments. Obviously, Josh has thought these things through.

Josh goes on, "The third thing is sports. I admit that I am not a very good baseball or football player. Although I like to watch those games, and track and field meets, and basketball games, I'd rather watch them then play them."

He took a deep breath, "Dad, my sport is cycling."

His dad shakes his head, this is not what he wants to hear, "Make your point, son."

Josh's well-thought-out plan pours out, "My friend, Ron Thomas and I have been biking together on the weekends whenever the weather is good. We are in good shape and have been talking about taking a longer ride this summer with some overnights. We want to push our distance out to a few hundred miles."

Josh opens his well-used map on the work bench and shows his Dad his proposed route that he has traced across the mountains north of Argyle. "Remember when we went on a family vacation near Yosemite a couple of years ago?"

"A good part of our bike trip will take us up that way. We'll stick to quiet side roads so traffic won't be a problem.

"We are thinking about taking about three weeks to ride out and back. We'd leave the first Monday of after school is out.

"I have talked with Mr. Steeler and he is okay with my plan. In fact, whether or not I take this ride, Mr. Steeler wants his son to take over for me for the summer, so he won't need me. I have arranged for some buddies to take over my yard work while I'm gone.

"I've saved some more than enough for the trip. It'll be pretty cheap since we'll be camping out. Ron and I will have racks on our bikes to carry our sleeping bags and other gear. We'll stay in public campgrounds; I've marked them with X's on this map.

I have my smart phone, thanks to you. I'll keep it charged and call home every evening to let you know where we are and how we're doing and …"

Raising his hands, his dad interrupts Josh's enthusiastic description of the trip, "Whoa! Whoa! Slow down! Let me absorb some of this. I haven't met Ron Thomas. Who is he?"

"A buddy from school. He's kind of like me – almost a junior; doesn't do a lot of team sports but likes biking. We ride together all the time. He is in good shape and ready to go."

"What do his parents think about this trip?"

"Ron has gotten their OK."

Josh's dad would rather his youngest son played football or baseball on local HS fields than traipse all over the mountains of the Sierra Nevada. He looks out of the window of the garage, considering Josh's request. His mind is turning over. He smiles at himself. He's learning about some surprisingly good qualities in his youngest son.

Josh is way different than Ed is, that's for sure. Bob has been hammering on Josh to grow up. Well, evidently, that is just what he has been doing—on his own terms. Yes, his grades are a bit better and he has a better job, but now – now he wants to pedal his fool bike on this very long trip. It sounds a bit crazy to him. He finally looks up at Josh and says, "I'm not sure about this. Let me think about it and talk it over with your mom."

Late that evening, Bob and his wife had just gone to bed for the night when he tells her about Josh's proposed trip. Lynn was quiet at first, but then the questions came pouring out. "Bob, is it safe? Are they old enough to do that kind of trip? Are they in good enough shape? Are you convinced they've planned it well?"

He rubs his hand across his forehead. "I have been asking the same questions, Lynn. One thing I can say is that he is completely invested in the trip. I think that he wants to prove something to himself and to us."

Tears were in her eyes. How quickly her youngest is changing.

Bob reached for her hand. "Don't worry, Lynn. We'll figure this out.

"You know that, to me, cycling has never seemed like the sport for him. I'm sure he could learn more from team sports … something different than riding his bicycle all day.

"To tell the truth, my first impression of Josh's plan for his trip was that it is a wild proposal. But, since then, I've given it some more thought. It would be an important learning experience for him. The trip should be safe enough. We have all camped out plenty of times, so he knows what he is doing there. And, I have to admit, he does know something about bikes."

Bob slowly shakes his head, "But I have doubts that the trip will go the way that he and his buddy have planned it. They are about to discover the real problems with pedaling long distances, especially with the heavy loads they will be carrying. Add to that, camping out every night. It will be a hard lesson.

"Josh's past bike rides with his buddy have all been one-day trips, not more than 30 miles or so. When they start riding all day for many days on this trip, pushing much longer distances and climbing some steep roads in the Sierra Nevada, the ride will become tough – much tougher than anything they have done before.

"Frankly, I think they'll turn around and be back in our garage in three or four days, if not sooner. They will be disappointed, but it will be a good lesson for Josh. Perhaps, then, he will start to listen to us."

Lynn is quiet for a few seconds, putting her hands over her face. Then she turns to Bob and asks, "What if you are wrong? What if they keep going?"

He smiles knowingly, "They won't. The only other possibility is that after a couple of tough days on the road and some uncomfortable camping, Joshua will give us a call asking for a pick up."

The next day, Josh gets the approval for the trip from his parents. He can tell that they are a bit hesitant, but he still gets the go-ahead.

His dad continues to ask for more details about the trip, especially the plans for first few days. Josh is happy to inform him and give him a copy of the map with the route marked on it."

9.

Josh and Kelly see each other often. Neither considers their meetings as dates, although their conversations have become very easy, especially when they stand for a few minutes under their favorite tree. They share campus happenings and discuss homework, asking each other questions and listening carefully to the answers. They talk about family. They talk about classes. Kelly's grasp of math and science and her ability to make those subjects clear helps Josh a lot. There is a growing trust between them.

Now that the bike trip is going to happen, today, he meets her under their tree to share his plans. The tree is beautiful. Kelly and Josh are shaded by its drooping limbs heavy with leaves and hard, green walnuts.

Josh enthusiastically describes the trip, pulling maps up on his smart-phone to show her the details. Kelly is excited for him, but at the same time, she also feels a bit sad. "Josh, how long? Four weeks? That … that seems forever!"

Kelly is surprised at her own reaction. A bit embarrassed to have her feelings out in the open, she looks down for a second and shakes her head, trying to clear away the sadness. Then she looks up at Josh, giving him her best smile despite tiny tears in the corners of her eyes.

"When are you and Ron leaving?"

"The Monday after school is out for the summer," Josh replies, clearly excitedly at just the thought of it. "Ron and I are going crazy with organization. This is a way bigger trip than we have ever tried." He laughed, "In my log book, I am calling it **'The Great Adventure!'**

Heading back to classes, Josh continues to give Kelly more details about his summer adventure. They talk about some of the problems he is having with his family and she knows how important it is for him to get away from home for awhile

Final preparations for the trip are hectic for Josh, squeezed in between studying for exams, wrapping up his lawn jobs and his final days working for Mr. Steeler for the summer. And then, suddenly, all his efforts seemed to be for nothing.

Only a few days before classes end and the start of the bike trip, Josh hurries to one of his last classes, dodging other students rushing down the hallways. He is brought to a sudden halt when a hand reaches out of the crowd and grabs his arm. It's Ron. He raises his voice to be heard above the noise, shouting into Josh's face, "I have to talk to you! I have a big problem."

They step into a side-corridor that is barely quieter. Clearly, Ron is upset. "This is hard to say, but I won't be going on our trip."

Josh squints at Ron and shouts a reply. "What? I don't think I heard you right. Say that again."

Ron looks up, speaking loudly, "I can't go on our trip."

Josh is surprised – almost speechless – as he processes Ron's words. "Ron, I'm not sure I'm hearing you. C'mon outside."

They squeeze through the mob of students to an exit and standing off the sidewalk. Josh asks Ron to tell him again.

Ron takes a deep breath and says, "I can't go on our trip."

Josh scratches his head. He is mystified at this sudden announcement. If he has heard Ron correctly, a lot of preparation for a great will go down the drain. "Ron, I don't understand. Everything is ready to go. We're almost packed. What's the problem?"

Ron becomes a little emotional, not able to look directly at Josh. Then he explains. "It's my Mom. She's sick. She has to have an operation and then there'll be a long time getting better. I'm the oldest. I have to help Dad with my brother and little sister."

There are a few moments of silence while Josh considers this sad and disappointing news. Finally, he looks up at his friend, "Ron, you have to help your folks now. As for our bike trip, there will be another time. Don't worry."

"What will you do, Josh?"

Josh rubs the back of his head, "I'm not sure. I'll probably just put it off."

Reaching out, he puts a hand on his friend's shoulder. Don't worry about me, Ron. Do what you have to. Your family needs you."

10.

Kelly and Josh sit on the grass, facing each other in the shade of their tree. The shade and light breeze are a relief from the hot, late spring sun. Kelly is very happy that the semester is ending, excitedly telling Josh about her new summer job. She'll be working a few hours a week at a small book store.

"Josh, they sell e-books and printed books and many used books. And since I'll be working there, I can buy them for almost nothing. Some great reading fun ahead for the summer!"

She went on talking about her summer job when she notices that Josh is only half-listening. With a questioning smile, she says, "Hello … Josh? Are you there?"

Shaking his head, he apologizes, "Sorry, Kelly, there are just a couple of things buzzing around in my brain." He smiled, concentrating on her pretty face. "Your bookstore job sounds good. If you see any books on biking, grab them for me!"

Kelly knows that something is wrong. She reaches over and touches his arm and asks, "Josh, what's bothering you?"

He doesn't answer for a few seconds, looking up at the blue sky, thinking. Then he tells her.

"Kelly, I need to tell you about a change in my bike trip plan. It's big. I haven't talked to anyone else about this, but I need to tell someone I trust—that's you. Tell me what you think."

Kelly is surprised. Frowning at Josh, she nudges his knee with hers, "What in the world are you up to now, Joshua?"

"You know that my buddy, Ron Thomas, and I have been planning our summer bike trip all spring. We are almost packed and ready to go."

Nervously looking down, Josh pulls at tufts of grass as he talks. "But now, a big problem has come up."

He stops and takes a deep breath then tells Kelly the worst. "Ron's mom is sick and he has to back out of our trip."

Putting her hand to her mouth, Kelly frowns at the news. "Oh no!" She reaches out to touch Josh's arm. "Oh no! What is the problem with his mother?"

Kelly can feel Josh's disappointment. She wants to hug him— to tell him not to worry … that everything will be OK.

Josh explains as well as he can.

Kelly listens intently, reflecting both her personal concern and a desire, someday, to follow in her mother's medical footsteps.

She shakes her head, "It sounds very serious. I hope she'll be alright.

"And Josh, I'm really, really sorry that your trip is off."

Josh is quiet for a minute. He self-consciously looks away from Kelly, not sure how to tell her what he is going to do. In a whisper, she asks, "Have you told your parents?"

He doesn't respond at first. He works to get his thoughts together as he pulls up a few blades of the grass and rolls them between his fingers. Finally, he takes a deep breath and looks up at her, the seriousness of his decision showing on his face. He begins to tell Kelly about his new plans. "Kelly, you know that I've had a big problem with my parents for the last few months. They are really starting to drive me up the wall! We have been on the outs for weeks. I need this trip to get away, to get some room to be … to be … to be me!

"My parents just don't understand me! They think that I should be a younger version of my older brother, Ed. I tell them that we are different. I do my own thing – and do it pretty well. But they don't like my choices, they think Ed's way is the answer."

She can see and see and hear Josh's anger. He frowns and raises his voice, almost yelling, "My performance in school is never good enough for them and Dad says that my cycling is just an excuse for not doing 'real' sports. Whatever I do, there is something wrong with it!"

Josh rubs his eyes. "Then finally – FINALLY! They said I could take this bike trip with Ron. I was so ready to go, but now, without Ron …"

He is quiet for minute, gathering his thoughts. He finally says, "I have made up my mind, Kelly. I'm still going to go on the bike trip. The only difference is that I'll go alone. Call it running away from home or whatever, I'm still going to do it."

There is a look in Josh's eyes that Kelly hadn't seen before. She has no question about his determination as he explains his new plan to her.

"And one more thing. Ron and I had planned our trip to take about three weeks. I think that my solo trip will be longer. I just won't tell my parents 'til I'm way down the road."

Kelly closes her eyes and hugs her knees as she sits on the grass. Finally, she Looks up at Josh, wanting to help him make it his plan work. She asks, "Won't your mom and dad call Ron's parents at some point?"

Josh had thought about that and he is quick to answer, "They don't know each other. Besides, with my brother graduating and getting ready for college, they aren't focused on my activities. I doubt that they would even remember Ron's last name."

Josh shakes his head stubbornly. "Anyway, that doesn't matter. I'm going to do it! Sure, I will let them know where I am at some point. But, between now and then, I have to get away from home – far away.

Josh and Kelly sit quietly on the grass for a few more minutes. His determination softens briefly as he looks into her eyes. He leans over to her and whispers, "The only bad thing is that I won't be able to see you while I'm on the road, Kelly."

The moment ended abruptly as the bell rang calling them back to class. They stood, facing each other for another few seconds as Kelly gave Josh a resigned smile. He was strong. Taking his hand in both of hers, she looked into his eyes speaking in a whisper. "Josh, I don't know what to say except that I will really, really miss you."

"Me, too – you," he said.

They quietly reflect on the words they've just exchanged. They seem to have more meaning than either had expected.

Kelly asks, "When will you go?"

"I'll leave the same day that Ron and I had picked, Monday after school is out."

"To tell the truth, I'd like to leave tomorrow, but my brother, Ed, is graduating on Saturday and my parents are throwing a big party—its family stuff." Josh shakes his head and gives a resigned shrug.

"As little as we talk, Ed and I could be on separate planets. And the few times we do talk, he speaks in put-downs. His party sure won't be my favorite place to be, but it's a special family thing and I have to be there."

She asks for more details about his trip. Kelly is impressed with Josh's organization. He might have had a little trouble with geometry homework, but his planning skills are impressive. Pushing her eyeglasses up on her nose one more time, she looks him and asks, "Where will you go?"

"I'm heading into the mountains—the eastern Sierra. I know that area from family camping trips. I'll start on the same route Ron and I had planned. I'll show you the map before I go."

"Kelly, I have to tell you that a big difference with our original plan is that, when I reach what was to be the turn-a-round for Ron and me—I just might keep going."

Kelly wrinkles her brow. "I don't understand. You MIGHT KEEP GOING? Where? For how long? – Why?"

The thought about making the trip longer had been boiling inside of Josh since Ron told him he couldn't go. He knows that going alone is a reaction to his dad's attitude about Josh's biking efforts—this trip in particular. Without Ron, he will do what he wants.

Josh stares at the ground for a second. He hadn't given this new idea of extending his trip the attention he had given to the rest of his planning. He probably shouldn't have mentioned it to Kelly.

He looks up at this girl who means more to him every day—this girl who he doesn't really want to leave. "Kelly, I don't mean to worry you. Yeah, I have to admit that I haven't done any real planning for a longer trip. I just want you to know that the idea is whirling around in my brain. I am thinking seriously about it.

"I won't make a decision until I get out on the road for a week or so. You'll be the first one to know. But right now, I just need some time to get away from home, to think."

"I can tell you that I will start out in the same direction Ron and I had planned—north, into the Sierra Nevada Mountains. From there? We'll see.

"Kelly, you can be sure that whatever I do, I will come back to you."

He blushes when he realizes that he has just made a commitment to her. With widening blue eyes, Kelly has heard him clearly.

Josh stammers, "I … I will … I will try to call or text you every night. Sometimes the reception on my smart-phone will be bad or I won't be able to charge it where I camp. I promise to call you whenever I can.

"And, Kelly, please don't worry about me. I've saved some money and I have enough cash for a month or so. If I stay on the road longer, I'll look for a part-time job. The one thing that is for sure of is that I am going. You know that I have done a lot of biking. I can do this."

Kelly stands quietly, looking at Josh. She gives him one of her sweet 'hand-in-front-of-the-braces' smiles and shakes her head. "Josh, I know I'm going to miss you a lot and I'll worry about you, but I know that you will come back so I can hold your hand again. I … I think I love you!"

Surprised at her own words and suddenly shy, Kelly brings her hands to her face, blushing as tears of happiness and sadness run down her freckled cheeks.

Josh is taken back by that word, 'love.' He swallows nervously, his face becoming a bright red as he struggles for words. He finally stutters, "Ah … well … me too! Kelly, I promise to stay in touch. I will call you every day … I …"

The second bell calling the students to classes suddenly rings loudly, interrupting their conversation. They slowly walk back toward the school building holding hands, finally slipping them apart as they step into the crowd of noisy students rushing through the hallways.

11.

E d's big day is what Josh had expected. All of the attention is on his brother; his graduation honors, and his college plans. The graduation party that Bob and Lynn Mayer throw for their son the evening after the ceremonies is huge, attended by many of Ed's friends and their parents. The dining room table overflows with gifts and the house is filled with conversation and laughter. Josh hangs out on the periphery of the crowd and slips out to the garage to go over his trip checklist one more time. He is ready.

There are two departures from the Mayer household in the next few days. Josh's parents are focused on Ed, who has been accepted at the University of Colorado. It looks like Ed will major in business, following his dad's lead. They leave on Monday to fly to Colorado for a week for registration, an early tour of the campus, and a look into housing for the fall term.

The other departure, a couple of days later, is when Josh starts his bike trip. He's ready. He has covered all of his pre-trip responsibilities, including handing over his shop tasks to Mr. Steeler's son in the previous week. He couldn't help smiling when he walked out of the shop the last time for the summer—Steeler's son is going to have a great time taking over Josh's dirty work.

Otherwise, his lawn jobs are covered, too. He has introduced the guys taking them over to each of his customers, and showed his replacements the details special to each job.

Those tasks taken care of, his focus is now his last-minute trip preparations including packing, lists of contacts, money, and food for the first day or so on the road. Most importantly, he sees Kelly whenever he can.

She is busy, too. When summer vacation started, she took on two jobs. In addition to her bookstore work, with her Mom's advice, Kelly has set up a morning nursery for three five-year-old kids. She is good at organization and loves the kids. Dreams of being a pediatrician are often in her head.

Kelly and Josh manage to meet a couple of times a week at a local fast food restaurant, despite both of their hectic schedules. They sit at the counter talking and laughing about silly things. Or they just look shyly at each other while the ice melts in their unfinished soft drinks. Then it is back to work for Kelly and back to last-minute trip preparations for Josh.

✶✶✶

On the morning of his departure, he sits at the breakfast table saying goodbye to his parents. His dad, still in his robe, eyes his son sleepily. "Josh, you know that you must report to us every day. We will worry."

Josh's mind is racing with his thoughts of getting away from his parents' and their lack of understanding. He isn't his brother, he isn't his father. He is … he is who he is.

He smiles to his parents, waving his new smart phone. "Not to worry, Dad, thanks to this, I will be in regular contact!" he hugs his mom and shakes hands with his dad, promising again to stay in touch. They stand at the door as he throws his leg over his packed bike. He looks back at them with one last wave then pedals away.

Josh and Kelly had arranged to meet on the edge of the empty high school campus under their tree on his way out of town. The tree is heavy with new green walnuts. Dappled sunlight reaches the ground through the thick leaves moving gently in the light morning breeze. Beyond the tree, the sky is very blue – signs of a good day ahead.

At first, he doesn't see Kelly. Then, just as he thought she might not have come, she steps out of the shadows, sleepy-eyed and smiling beneath the tangle of her curly red locks.

Josh leans his packed bike against the trunk of their tree and walks up to her for what he knew would be the last time for quite a while. Even though this trip is the biggest thing he has ever done, Kelly is constantly in his thoughts. Josh just can't explain it to himself. He tries. Yes, she is so nice, so pretty, so understanding — but they are just friends.

She holds her glasses and pushes back the curls falling over her forehead with one hand and reaches out with her other to touch Josh's arm.

Kelly whispered, "Josh, I will miss you so … so much."

He touches her face then leans forward to kiss her.

She hesitates and turns slightly away with her fingers touching her lips, "But my braces …"

He tenderly pulls her hand away, quietly saying, "I know, Kelly." He kisses her cheek gently, then softly touches his lips to hers. After a few seconds, they slowly back away from each other. With tears dropping down her freckled cheeks, she inhales deeply and blurts out, "Oh Josh, I love you!"

He stammers, "And I – you, Kelly."

They move apart, amazed and enchanted at what has just happened. Josh moves slowly towards his bike, still looking at Kelly. With a hint of a smile, she holds her clasped hands under her chin, watching him. More words aren't possible—aren't necessary.

A minute later, the silence of the early morning is only broken by the sound of Josh's tires as he peddles down the gravel path to the road. Glancing back at Kelly, he waves one last time.

12.

Despite his early morning start, Josh has to navigate some busy roads out of Argyle. A little after 8 AM, he reaches Jones Valley Highway, a quiet two-lane road into the mountains north of the L.A. Basin. Traffic noise decreases dramatically as he climbs into the foothills but the mid-June heat increases. By ten o'clock he is at about the 2500 feet level, bathed in sweat. Most of the groundcover along the road is low-growing manzanita and other scrub brush. Shade is scarce.

He stops at a steep overlook to take a drink from his canteen. Looking back, he is happy to see that the LA sprawl with its smog and crazy traffic is finally behind him. In the other direction he can see bluer skies.

Back on his heavily loaded bike, he promises himself that "It will get better."

The hard climb seems to calm Josh down after his emotional good-bye to Kelly. He focuses on the trip ahead of him. This climb is only the first of what will be many up-hill slogs to come. Things will be easier as he gets into better shape in the next few days.

A half-hour later, he stands on in his pedals to get himself up one particularly steep piece of the road. The effort is worth it when he tops the crest to glide down a long downhill section. He shouts as he leans low over his handlebars "Way to go, Josh baby! Fly on down!"

He is soon back in his climbing mode – on his way up to Elgar pass. Compared to the ridges he had to cross the first 33 miles of his trip, this one is the steepest. Up, up, and more up. It seems to go on forever. One benefit, is that the temperature is falling, thanks to the increasing elevation. Beyond the 4,000-foot marker, a light breeze and the afternoon shade from thick stands of lodge pole pines along the road make things a lot more comfortable.

Josh can no longer see any evidence of the smoky LA Basin. Occasional views through the trees reveal clear mountain valleys below. He stops a couple of times to take pictures with his smart phone. Then he is back to climbing.

His concentration on the steep road is suddenly broken when a couple of deer bound out of the forest. They stop for a second to look at Josh, then run across the road to disappear into the trees and bushes. He thought briefly of taking a photo, but they were gone before he can reach for his smart phone. Josh shakes his head with a smile. He wishes he could ride at just half their speed!

Josh's log book would later reflect that, besides the steep climbing at this early stage, a lot of sharp switchbacks kept his attention. For some reason, the ones that turn up to his left seem particularly nasty with sharper curves and steeper climbs.

Traffic is light. A few slow-moving trucks give him lots of room and often give him friendly greetings as they pass. Of course, there is the occasional fast driving, less friendly driver, or other drivers just not paying attention—traveling too fast for the curves. After all his rides around Argyle, it isn't anything new. The small mirror he had on his handlebars saves him from close calls more than once.

About 4 p.m., Josh finally reaches Elgar Pass at an elevation of 5300 feet. He takes a long break to gulp down some water and a candy bar. He is more than 40 miles from home – a distance already beyond his weekend rides with Ron. He has to admit that he can feel it in his aching legs. Even his neck and back are a little sore. Those twice-a-week, flat highway 25-30-milers had barely gotten him in shape for this trip. He laughs at himself, yelling at the trees, "I'll sleep tonight!"

On the other side of the pass, for a few minutes, he enjoys a fast, 3-mile downhill ride that pushes forty miles an hour. That is over too soon when he flies over a bridge at the base of a narrow valley.

He sees a fast-moving mountain creek below, and stops quickly, to turn around and coast back to the bridge. He leans his bike against a skinny Lodge Pole Pine, and scrambles down to sit by the bubbling stream. Pulling off his shoes and sweaty socks, he dips his feet into the cold water with a loud, "AAhhh!"—startling a nearby flock of crows.

The driver of a passing 10-wheeler slowed enough to honk and wave at the cyclist lying comfortably on a large rock overhanging the creek.

About a half hour later, Josh is back on his bike, refreshed and climbing the last 9 miles to his first campsite. He makes it by a little after 5pm. He rides slowly through the camp entrance. It appears that this place is just a stop for travelers to use the rest room and fill up on water. No ranger, no store. Just a name and a reminder on a single sign posted at the campground entrance: "Henderson Flats Campground. Help us keep it clean."

He rides slowly around the boundary of the small parking lot looking for a place to set up camp for the night. Henderson Flats is empty – not a single tent or trailer or camper-van to be seen. Josh reasons that maybe is just too early in the season for many campers. Anyway, he doesn't need company. He's too tired to even think about talking to someone and this looks like a nice, quiet place to stay.

He was going to skip putting up his tent but a glance at the sky suggests some worrisome weather for the night with heavy clouds moving in from the west. Fifteen minutes later, his tent is up and his bike and saddlebags are jammed inside, next to his sleeping bag. It's a little tight, but he can still stretch out as long as he doesn't roll around much.

He fills his water bottles at a nearby faucet, then pulls together a simple 'can-of-beans' meal. It is cold, but good—especially when he tops it off with an apple, a candy bar and plenty of water.

Josh walks around a bit to stretch his legs. A cool evening breeze flows down the mountainside, moaning softly through the pine trees. Sleep will be refreshing here and welcome after all the tensions and sleepless nights at home before he left. But first, he has a couple of tasks.

He sits under a tall, pine tree on one of the benches that dot the campground and opens his bike diary.

Josh has kept a record of every trip he and Ron ever took. Entries are usually short, mostly just the date, riding time, and distance. There wasn't much about where they went because they took the same routes so often. This trip is different and he has promised himself to keep a more detailed log.

He sits down at a nearby camp table with a small spiral notebook in front of him and a pencil in hand. Mileage this first day was 55 miles. That is great. Twenty miles farther than the farthest Sunday ride with Ron. He had left Argyle about 6:30AM and pedaled into Henderson Flats ten and a half hours later. Whew … a long day with many stops. Although his actual riding time is probably closer to seven hours, even allowing for long stops, his average speed is slow. The culprits, of course, are those steep climbs.

He writes in his diary "The climb to Elgar Pass was the hardest I have ever attempted."

In fact, he had thought about walking it. But that wasn't him. If he had to ride a hill at 5mph, he did it. The old 'slow-but-sure' approach beats walking by a long shot.

Josh is proud of himself. This first day was the toughest ride he had ever attempted and he made it! For just a second, he recalls his dad's criticism of his biking. Then he chuckles at the thought of his brother, Ed, struggling up Elgar Pass. He adds another note to his diary, "It was my best hill – ever!"

When he stands up to walk back to his tent, he notices the flip side of his excitement about conquering his 'best hill ever'— he is tired. The climbs and the distance were made even harder because is hauling a heavy load on his old metal bike: sleeping bag, tent, water bottles, and saddle bags full of food, tools, and other gear. He smiles at the thought – it was probably too much. But he is pleased with his progress, sure that he'll be faster down the road as he gets into better shape. For now, he is happy just to stretch out on his sleeping bag and relax his aching legs.

An attempt to call home as the sun was setting brought no answer. He left a brief text message – just something to put off any worry, although he seriously doubted that there would be any.

Next, he sends a text to Kelly. Her encouraging smile was in his head when he climbed those tough hills back there and he wanted to tell her so. But it wasn't to be, at least not tonight. His connection to the net had died. He glares at his phone. He will try tomorrow.

He tends a blister on his right thumb by flashlight, then finally climbs into his sleeping bag with a thought that he would look at his map—planning for the next day. He was asleep as soon as he put his head down.

The next morning, Josh awakes at first light. He can smell the wet ground outside. He pushes the tent flap aside to see a drenched campground. Yes, his tent had proved to be a good idea despite the extra tired minutes it took to put it up.

He crawls outside and slowly stands, stepping around some puddles. He is a stiff, especially his legs. Some crows watch him from a nearby tree, giving their opinion in loud squawks. Josh waves a morning hello to the birds as he takes a few stretches in the fresh morning air. The weather is beautiful under clearing skies.

Josh investigates the outdoor shower just outside the restroom. He wrinkles his nose at what he calls his 'ripeness,' but shivers a bit when he thinks of stepping into the shower – cold water only.

He finally says, "What the hell!" and strips down to step into the very cold water. He later describes his experience in his diary as "A high-speed-shower: get wet, soap up, rinse off, and get out!" It might have taken a minute. Whether he is any cleaner is debatable. The important thing for him was that he feels cleaner as he towels off.

Josh dresses quickly in his bike shorts and shirt and a light sweatshirt. The dry, cool breeze makes him shiver. He checks his cellphone. No messages. Reception is still not very good, only a few bars of reception showed up. It was better than last night and he managed to get a couple of texts off to Kelly and to his parents.

Josh's simple breakfast consists of an apple, a handful of raisins, a mammoth-size peanut butter and jam sandwich and lots of water. Tent, sleeping bag, and other clothes and equipment are then quickly packed.

He takes good advantage of the location of Henderson Flats near the top of a long hill and the cool morning breeze that rolls down the mountain slope behind him. He flies down the empty road flanked by the ever-present pines. The invigorating smell of the forest and the sound of the wind whistling through his bike helmet seems to wash all the issues of family and school out of his head. Yes, he is a little sore, but he feels free, doing what he wants to do. It's a great morning.

13.

J osh is in better shape. There are still a few aches and pains when he climbs back on his bike the next morning, but those are almost gone. After three days and 165 miles of pedaling, Josh is now well into that towering California mountain range, the Sierra Nevada, located on the eastern side of the state.

The road he is traveling is mostly on the eastern slopes, a few thousand feet below the crests of the mountains. Lodge Pole Pine and Aspen shade much of his path. Above the tree line, on the shaded sides of a few of the highest peaks, he can see patches of snow.

Occasionally he stops at a break in the trees for a view of the arid land well below him to the east. That is the edge of Death Valley. He is glad to be at a much cooler, high elevation.

The traffic is light. Aside from the occasional ten-wheeler lumbering by, his company has only been a few soaring hawks, a squirrel or two, and a few curious deer. One wide-eyed fawn slowly walks by, taking a curious look at Josh. He stops to reach for his smart phone for a picture, only to be disappointed when the deer suddenly bounds away.

Toward the middle of the morning, the highway traffic becomes much heavier. Trucks carrying construction equipment roar past him. On a few occasions he has to stop on the shoulder of the road to let some larger loads go by. Even when it is finally safe to ride, the line of trucks is still long, noisy, and smoky.

Josh pulls onto the shoulder and stops at an intersection of the main highway with what appears to be a quiet side road that branches eastward. It's empty for as far as he could see. The lack of traffic would be a nice change.

He checks his location on his smart-phone. Poor reception. Unfolding his paper road map, with its sketchy details, he notices that he is close to a side road that takes a short detour to the east then turns northward to parallel the highway he is on now. Perfect. No heavy traffic going that way.

Josh still isn't absolutely sure that this is the correct road. He stands there for a few minutes, trying to make his mind up when another heavy truck belching black smoke groans loudly up the hill behind him. That's enough. He'll check out the side road.

Josh swallows a handful of peanuts and takes a few gulps of water from his canteen before he jumps on his bike to enjoy what seems to be a great ride. Absolutely no traffic and downhill. Coasting rapidly away from the main highway, he relaxes as his bike accelerates to 30 miles an hour.

It isn't long before he begins to have second thoughts. Fast and quiet, yes, but after 45 minutes, he realizes his so-called short-cut is taking him too far east towards a hotter, much drier area – towards the desert. The pines that had been giving him protection from the wind and sun quickly give way to thick sage brush below the tree line. He stops to check his location.

Josh leans against his bike on the shoulder of the desolate road and he squints into the June sun. Exactly, where is he? A hot wind gust rustles the tufts of blond hair poking out of his bike helmet. The downhill had been great – fast and fun – for a while. But now, the desert-like surroundings are unsettling. Where is he?

The reception on his smart-phone was weak at his last stop and has gotten worse. There is definitely no access to the net from his location. His navigation system now amounts to his odometer and an old roadmap. He has to figure out where he is or he'll be sleeping in the sagebrush come nightfall.

He opens his map across his handlebars when a sudden gust of wind suddenly rips it out of his hands. "Oh, No!" He drops his bike to chase it down. Too late. The strong wind, rough terrain, and thick brush are too much, the map is gone. Josh stops running and shouts at the empty sky, "Damn! What the hell else can go wrong?"

He kicks his wheel and keeps yelling his frustrations into the hot wind until he is nearly hoarse. He finally stops shouting and shakes his head He takes a deep breath and talks a bit more calmly to himself, "C'mon Josh, you got down here, you can get back to where you started. Quit moaning!"

He turns around to retrace his route.

The great downhill ride he experienced just an hour ago turns into a lousy, hard, slow, uphill pull. By five pm, Josh's morning high about being in better shape is long gone. The next campground should have only been 45 miles from when he started his day. An easy distance, if he hadn't gotten off-track – 18 lousy miles off-track. And he gave up more than 3,000 feet in altitude. The price of that quick descent is a tough, slow climb back up into the forest.

A sweaty two hours later, he begins to see a few pine trees. Their occasional shade gives him a welcome reprieve to the hot sun. The forest is thicker after another half hour of climbing. Josh's popping ears tell him that he has gained back a lot of altitude. He pushes his bike around a thick stand of trees. He is back to the main highway.

Josh stops with a sigh of relief and looks up and down the highway. The road is empty. The traffic that had been the reason for his detour in the first place is gone. He shakes his head and knocks his fist against his bike helmet, loudly talking to himself "Josh, you idiot, you should have just taken a rest and waited for the heavy truck traffic to clear. Damn! Now you are tired and nowhere near the next campground!"

He mounts his bike and heads off over some rolling ridges— nothing like the hill he had just climbed. Fifteen miles later, he wheels up to the entrance of his next campsite. "Lost Hills Camp." He chuckles at the name. It sure fits his day wandering around.

It is late. The sun is already close to the mountains tops and long shadows are falling from the tallest peaks. Josh checks his odometer. His total distance for the day was 81 miles. That is good—his best daily distance so far. On the other hand, he is ticked off at himself for mistakenly taking that detour back there. He is really only a little over 45 miles from last night's campground.

The ranger on duty is standing at the camp entrance as Josh stepped off his bike. "Hi cyclist! You're lucky, I am just closing the campground for evening. You just made it."

Josh stumbles unclipping himself from his pedals causing his heavy load of tent and saddle bags to pull the bike over until it lay on the ground between his legs. He stands there for a moment, and looks down. He is almost too tired to move. Finally, he steps over the bike and looks up at the ranger. With an embarrassed smile and a headshake, he simply says, "Long day."

It is obvious to the ranger that the young cyclist is exhausted and probably hadn't had a good meal in a while. He had a few questions. "What's your name, son? Where are you from? How long have you been on the road? Where are you going?"

Josh introduces himself with a handshake and patiently recounts his ride, explaining that today's ride was a little longer because he had taken the wrong road. He stretches his arms and yawns. "I'm just a bit tired."

The ranger is fascinated by this skinny young kid. Josh seems to be a lot of what he wants to see in his own young sons: smart, adventurous, careful – to a point – and persistent when the going got tough. He can't help but like Josh even though he didn't really know him.

He looked at Josh's obviously slight build and asked, "When was your last meal?"

Josh laughed, "One thing you can be sure of is that I eat – a lot and often. Today wasn't any different—a good lunch and snacks along the way."

Next, came the question Josh was waiting for, "How old are you? You look a bit young to bite off a trip like this."

Skipping around his age, Josh assures the ranger that cycling was not unusual for him. "I have a good bike and I've ridden a lot of miles getting ready for this trip.

"I'm a little worn out after my detour today, but a good night's sleep will fix me up."

He could tell that the ranger was truly interested, not only in his trip, but also in his safety.

"Does anyone know you're out here?"

"I have a smart phone so I can have regular check-ins with my parents and some friends."

The conversation becomes more relaxed. The ranger gives Josh information about the campground. "Well you sound like you know what you are doing, kid. Here are a couple of forms to fill out. If you need some food, I can open the camp office for a few minutes."

Josh pays the camping fee and in exchange receives a campground brochure. It has a good local map. A good replacement for the one that the wind grabbed when he took his ill-advised detour back a lot of miles. Now he will have better information about the altitudes of the road in the area for his diary.

Josh takes the ranger up on his offer to open the store so he can replenish his dwindling food supplies. Afterwards, the ranger shows him the campsites and the locations of the toilets and showers. He said, "You can pick any site, the camp is empty tonight. Things won't get busy until around the July 4th weekend." He made a wide gesture toward the campground, "So you have it all to yourself!"

He waves goodnight to Josh as he locks the office behind him and makes his way to his own cabin. "Have a good night, kid."

Josh leans his bike next to a tree at a nearby campsite and decides to skip pitching his tent. The night is clear and a mattress of pine needles for his sleeping bag is all he needed. Taking a deep breath of the sweet smells of the forest, especially the pines, he can feel the stress of the day's ride slipping away. A good night's sleep will fix him up. But first there are contacts to be made.

To his dad, he texted his daily report, still being careful not to mention that he was riding alone. HI FOLKS STOPPING TONIGHT AT LOST HILLS CAMPGROUND NICE PLACE

GOOD FOOD ABOUT TO TURN IN RIDING IS GOOD GOTTA GO THIS IS JOSH HAVING FUN!

Before he turns off his smart phone, he tries to call Kelly. This would be the first time they talked since he left. There had been only a few brief texts.

She answers on the first ring. "Josh, I – I'm sooo happy to hear you! Where are you? Are you OK?"

At the sound of Kelly's voice, Josh's weariness washes away. He describes his day and the campground and assures her that he is doing just fine, getting in better shape and – "Kelly, I miss you – a lot!"

They were enthusiastically sharing details of their days when their connection begins to get weaker. Kelly's last comment is cut off. "Today, I …" then nothing.

He tries to reconnect with no success, "Damn phone!"

Since there are no other campers around, Josh runs over to the shower with his towel wrapped around his bare body and his clean clothes in his hand. The water is very cold and the shower is brief. His teeth chatter as he towels off. He could be cleaner, but the shower was "Better than nothing!"

He downs can of cold soup, an oatmeal-raisin cookie, and nearly a quart of milk. His dinner time is shared with a few stinging mosquitoes, reminding him to apply repellent. At last, he crawls into his sleeping bag. Despite the insects, he notices that he feels a bit more comfortable than when he camped at the earlier stops. He thought he was getting used to riding alone. He had never really thought much about being afraid, although now he realizes that having a ranger nearby is a good thing. He was fast asleep before dark.

14.

By the end of his eighth day on the road, Josh is disappointed with his progress. His daily riding distances haven't been as good as he'd like them to be. The culprit is the terrain—rugged, rolling roads. Yeah there have been some great fast descents – he hit 55mph on one – but the slow, hard climbs are taking their toll. He is worn out by nightfall.

His choices of campsites probably didn't help. Those places weren't exactly restful–wide spots in the woods on the edge of a deserted parking lots at a trail head or behind an isolated gas station. Late at night, some of those stops have been kind of spooky. Earlier on his trip, he camped at a spot thirty feet into the woods behind a large bill board. He figured it would keep the flashing headlights of passing trucks from disturbing his sleep. Although the weather was dry, he put up his tent as sort of a flimsy barrier between him and what he called the *night critters*.

Just as he was dozing off, a loud crash from a nearby stand of trees brought him out of his sleeping bag with a flashlight in one hand and his hunting knife in other. He swore that he heard something walking around out there—some ragged breathing. Wide-eyed for a while, he finally hunkered down around midnight for a few more restless hours of sleep.

The next morning, four deer stand quietly in the brush watching curiously as Josh takes his tent down and packs up between bites of his peanut butter sandwich and some loud swallows from a can of orange juice. When he pushes his bike to the road, the deer leap noiselessly away.

Out Of The Shadows and Into The Fire

With his interrupted sleep, he is starting late—after 9AM. Fortunately his planned ride is mercifully short, only about 40 miles. The road is rolling and, for a welcome change, none of the climbs are particularly steep. Fellow travelers are only a few lumber trucks with their huge loads of freshly cut trees and, once, a state trooper who taps his horn and waves as he drives by.

Josh takes more frequent stops for water and snacks to boost his energy. The effect isn't great. Despite the shorter, easier pedal to his next stop, he is slowing down. He needs a break.

A fast-moving pickup truck comes up behind Josh driving a little too close to the side of the road. Concentrating on his climbing effort, Josh only catches sight of the truck at the last moment. He turns his bike sharply onto the shoulder of the road where a patch of soft sand grabs his front wheel and pushes it in a direction where he doesn't want to go. With no time to detach his pedal clips, he goes down. Hard.

Maybe the driver wasn't paying attention; maybe Josh was hidden in the shadows of the thick pines; whatever the reason, it is a near disaster.

The truck is gone and Josh is in an uncomfortable twisted position on his right side. His right knee and elbow are stinging with bloody scrapes. His left foot has popped out of its shoe. It felt OK. But his right foot is a problem. It is still in its shoe clipped to the pedal. There is an ache in that ankle. Josh twists around in an effort to assess the damage. He can't turn enough to see the foot, yet he could tell that it is resting an uncomfortable angle. He sits up awkwardly to unclip his right foot when he suddenly hears a sound that makes him freeze.

It is a buzz—the buzz of a rattlesnake.

Josh rolls his head slowly and deliberately in the direction of the scary sound. He sees it. A snake is about 6 feet away. At least three feet long, its head is up and its rattles are shaking a warning as its beady eyes studied the fallen cyclist. Josh stays perfectly still. He is stuck. He knows he can't quickly untangle himself from his bike to get safely away.

Fifteen minutes later, then only thing that has changed is that Josh's right ankle is beginning to throb. The snake is still there. He thinks of throwing a something at it to chase it away. He very slowly looks around—no rocks close by. Even if he finds something to throw and he misses, he might have to deal with pissed off snake. Bad idea.

Time moves slowly. There is no breeze. The ground is hot and his mouth is very dry. Not taking his eyes off the snake, he reaches slowly for the water bottle clipped to his bike. He drains it.

A half hour later, the situation hasn't changed. Josh is still tangled up in his bike and the snake is still there, staring and giving warnings with sporadic rattles. Josh tries to stay alert in case the snake starts to move his way. He watches and watches, fighting his fatigue. He nods off.

Josh jerks awake! He thinks he had dozed for just a few seconds but a glance at his watch surprises him. It has been 20 minutes! He slowly rolls his head from side to side, scanning the area. He pulls himself up onto his elbows for a better view. The snake is gone.

He sits up stiffly and untangles himself from his bike, carefully using both hands to slip his aching foot out of his right shoe. He stands slowly, then spends a few minutes stretching to relieve his stiffness. His right ankle is a little sore but he can walk without limping. It's OK!

A few minutes later, Josh mounts his bike and rotates the pedals away slowly to test his ankle. It hurts some, but he will be able to pedal the eight miles or so to the next campground without any real problem. Back on his bike, the last few hills he has to climb are mercifully easy and well shaded.

His arrives at his next campsite later in the afternoon than he had originally planned. In his diary, he calls the reason for his long day "The Snake Delay."

Beaver Lake Campground is clean, uncrowded, and well located. Josh's weariness fades when he finally gets off his bike at the camp entrance. He takes a few minutes to gaze across the road at the reflection of trees and clouds in the calm waters of a beautiful blue lake. Distant mountains frame the view. He can feel a sense of relaxation—a sense of pride. He is here after a really tough day.

Shaded by a grove of huge Ponderosa pines, a few camper-vans and tents are scattered around the otherwise empty campground. Josh is ecstatic to finally stay in a campground with showers with hot and cold water. After his tough day, he feels that he is a little closer to civilization with other campers – company – nearby.

The entrance to an old wooden building that houses the camp office and a small store is marked by a tall pole with the American flag and the California State Flag waving in the breeze. Josh walks in to register. A park employee looks up from his desk, "Welcome to Beaver Lake, cyclist! I saw you pedal in. Looks like you are on quite a trip with that load you're carrying!"

Josh smiles at the recognition. "Hi. Thanks. I'm sure happy to be at this great place – the lake, the trees – the campgrounds. They are all a welcome change to some of the places back down the road where I pitched my tent." He laughs, "Showers with hot water! I can't wait."

Josh answers several questions about his trip, although he is a little vague about his destination. He is pleasantly surprised by the lack of any questions about his age. Maybe, with the grease and sweat marks on his bike clothes and his longer, uncombed hair— maybe he just looks older."

The fellow registering him announces, "I have a surprise for you! In celebration of National Cycling Week, we are waving registration fees for all cyclists!"

Josh is thrilled to be able to save $25. He walks over to the camp store to buy a few more supplies than his usual pork and beans. With an opened can of root beer in one hand and his bag of groceries balanced precariously on his handlebars, he pushes his bike to a flat, shaded campsite, where he sits on the ground and leans against the trunk of a huge pine tree.

Good food and a sound night's sleep fill his thoughts. As he begins to set up his camp, he decides that he is going to take a break and stay at Beaver Lake for an extra day. He finishes his dinner sitting on a large rock near the edge of his campsite.

Afterwards, he unpacks his bike. Relaxation creeps into his weary muscles while he puts his tent up. Pine needles under his sleeping bag soften his bed. He sits down and scratches a few notes in his diary while the setting sun reddens the nearby mountain peaks and ridges. Besides jotting down the usual numbers – distances and times, he writes about his infamous snake incident. It sends chills up his spine as he recalls the warning sound of the coiled rattlesnake.

He texts his parents, then Kelly, nearly falling asleep in mid-message. She came back with a short description of her busy day and her always special, MISS YOU JOSH!

The next morning is a good one for Josh. He had slept long and hard and feels great, especially knowing that this is a rest day for him. Just the thought of not riding for a day seems to refresh him. To top it off, Kelly sends a GOOD MORNING text that brings a smile to his face.

He tends to the business of minor scrapes, bruises, blisters and mosquito bites. The foot he twisted yesterday barely ached. Other than that, there is only a small purple bruise near the outside of his ankle.

After another good shower, he ducks back into his tent to tape a couple of old blisters and spread some sunscreen over exposed skin. His right forearm is a deep red where he missed a spot day before. He even remembers to put a can of mosquito repellant in his pocket. Josh laughs at his organization. His brain is working much better after that great sleep.

Outside his tent, josh stands to stretch his sore muscles while watching the rays of the rising sun spread over the mountains to the east. The sun finally shows its bright face, pushing all the long shadows behind the tall trees.

He is interrupted by a friendly voice, "Hey cyclist!"

The greeting comes from a tall, lean, dark-haired fellow, probably in his early thirties, tinkering with a bicycle in the adjoining campsite.

At a glance, it was clear to Josh that this guy is in terrific shape. Not an ounce of fat – anywhere! He has the build of an experienced cyclist – slim, that is, except for his legs. Josh would later describe him to Kelly: "The guy had 'thunder thighs!'"

His neighbor walks over to shake Josh's hand. "I'm Will Chang. You're probably surprised to see me here. When I pulled in last evening, it was already getting dark." He smiled, "From the snoring I heard, I think you were already asleep for the night."

Will takes off his sunglasses. He looks over Josh's equipment with a nod and a friendly grin. "Wow! It looks like you have enough gear for a long ride. Where are you going?"

It had been awhile since Josh rode with his buddy, Ron. A lot of riding alone. He is glad to talk to another cyclist – someone who knows what riding is all about -- someone who can talk 'bikes.'

"Hey Will, I'm Josh Mayer. "I'm pedaling up north from here. Started near LA. I will be going that way for another week or two then …" He hesitated because he wasn't sure, "… probably back again. Where have you been riding?"

Chang rubs his very black, short hair. His smile and easy manner instantly put Josh at ease. "Well, at this stage, my sore butt makes me feel like I have been everywhere! I'm on a cross-country ride. Been on the road for almost six weeks. Started in Wisconsin – Madison – then hopped over into Canada and tooled around the cold and windy plains, then back to the states through Montana with a squirrely route to here. I'm just about finished. I have a brother in San Diego. I'll fly back to Madison from there."

Josh no longer thinks about his own sore back and the tough parts of his trip. Will's tale is exciting. "Wow! What a ride!"

Josh leans over Will's bike for a closer inspection. He shakes his head in amazement, "Carbon fiber yes? Light and fast!"

Will nods, "Yep. It's one of the best I've ridden. No complaints." Then he asks Josh how his ride was going.

"Compared to you, I'm just poking along – I doubt that I could keep up with you for more than five minutes!"

Will shakes his head, "C'mon, Josh. You can't make comparisons like that. There are big differences, not only in our bikes, but in our loads and then there's our ages and experience. No, it's not fair to compare. I'll tell you this, when I was your age, I never tackled a ride like the one you are on now. No, it wasn't until a few years later.

"You are doing great!"

Josh is pleased with Will's assessment of his effort, but then Will asks him some tough questions, "Josh, what does the rest of your trip look like? How far north are you going? Are you riding back this way or taking another route?"

Will recognizes some hesitant body language in the younger cyclist. It is clear that Josh is uncertain or not ready for questions. The older cyclist frowns, wondering to himself what Josh plans to do.

Josh rubs his forehead as conflicting thoughts whirl around in his mind: missing Kelly, problems with his family, his jobs, and the next school year coming up at the end of the summer. All creep into his thoughts. Since he had left Argyle a couple of weeks ago, all of those worries gradually went away to be replaced by concentrating on climbing the next hill and deciding where he would sleep at the end of the day. Will's question about where he is going is a reality check. Is he really running away? Josh knows that that idea is now becoming questionable.

He looks back at Will. "To be honest, I'm not exactly sure … but I do plan to be back home by mid-August. I'll hit my turn-a-round in the next week or so."

Will isn't completely satisfied with Josh's answer. He asks, skeptically, "So, Josh, exactly where is that turn-a-round going to be, as you put it, 'In the next week or so'?"

Josh grins and points toward the beautiful view of Beaver Lake through the cluster of pine trees shading the camp. "This place is so beautiful, I think I could stay here and kick back here until it's time to go home, but I'm just not quite ready to stop. With a good rest today, tomorrow I'll be good for some more riding days up north. To be honest, I'm not quite sure how much longer I want to ride or how far I want to go."

He laughed, "I suppose when I really start missing my Mom's cooking, I'll be at my turn around point—I'll know when I get there."

Will shakes his head, a little frustrated at Josh's so-called plan. "I guess you know what you're doing and I can see that I'm not about to change your mind. Let's check out your bike."

Will kneels down and holds Josh's bicycle at arm's length, giving the wheels a visual inspection. He tugs on the chain; turns the crank; and checks the brakes. Then, with Josh holding the rear wheel off the ground, he goes through the gear changes.

He stands up, folding his arms. "So far, your bike looks like it's in good shape. It's just a little older and the weight is an issue, especially with the extra packs you are carrying. Sure, you're slower than I am, but there are trade-offs. The camping equipment, meals, tools, and sleeping bag you're hauling from campground to campground make you self-sufficient! You can stop anywhere."

Josh hadn't thought about the self-sufficient side of his trip. Will is right.

Will describes his own overnights with a laugh. "Yeah, I have camped a couple of times, but all I have is an ultra-light sleeping bag and a single, small saddle bag. Most of the time I stay in motels and eat out." He pats his belly and laughs. "My load is lighter and my food is better, Josh! But we really can't compare. You are the man, Josh! – doing the rugged ride!"

Will Chang uses his smartphone to show Josh maps of his trip and then, with Josh's guidance, lay out Josh's route from Argyle to Beaver Lake. Josh tells Will about his little side trip a few days ago. "I was stupid going off track so far, especially without directions. I might have gotten lost out there in the sagebrush."

The older, experienced cyclist finally asks to the question that Josh had been anticipating, "Josh, equipment aside, aren't you a bit young to be out here traveling alone?"

Josh grins at the question. "I hear that a lot. To you and a lot of other folks, I look young, but actually, I have done a lot of cycling. I'm in touch with my family; and, I'm … how did you put it? … Self-sufficient, right? I'm okay!"

They trade more stories about their rides, while Will makes some adjustments to Josh's gear and brake cables and talks to him about chain lubrication. He asks Josh about regular maintenance on his ride. "Too many riders work hard to get their bikes in shape before they leave, but when they get into their trip, regular maintenance falls off.

"The secret to minimizing problems is to check brakes, chains, and gearing every night. I assume you pump your tires regularly, right?"

"Yep, I do. I don't have a pressure gauge. I do a pretty good job judging the pressure with the old 'pinch test.'"

The older rider scratches his head. "Just a second, let me check my supplies."

A minute later, he returns and places a pressure gauge into the hand of a surprised Josh. "Wow! Thanks. What do I owe you?"

"It's a present; don't worry, I have another."

Will continues to inspect Josh's bike. "All-in-all, you have kept it in good shape, Josh. I don't know if it's a problem yet, but there is something going on in your rear wheel hub." He kneels next to the bike and shows Josh a very, very slight wobble in his rear wheel. "It's probably not noticeable when you ride."

Josh bends down for a closer look. "Oh, I see it now. It doesn't look like much."

Will shakes his head. "It's not good, Josh. I think it's your bearings. I had a similar problem at a critical point in a long ride a few years ago. I can tell you that it doesn't get better and the final result is that you walk."

Josh frowns, "That bad?"

Will nods and proceeds to explain the problem in detail. "Unfortunately, neither of us have the tools to pull the wheel apart. And, even if we did, we don't have the parts to fix it.

"I hate to say it, but you are probably only good for another day or so of hard riding – 100 miles at the most. Hopefully, in that distance, you can find a bike shop. Getting to one sooner than later is important."

Later the two cyclists share a cold meal sitting in front of Josh's tent, continuing to discuss the world of cycling. Josh has many questions that his new friend answers expertly.

Will also describes some of his other long rides, suggesting some good ones for Josh to consider in the future. "I think my favorite ride was New Zealand. The South Island. It was an amazing experience – beautiful country, great camps, and friendly, bike-smart people."

They talk for another half hour as the sun sinks in a beautiful display of mountain shadows and colorful clouds on the horizon. As the evening mountain breeze picks up, they shake hands, planning to meet over breakfast.

That evening, Josh lay in his tent thinking about his bike problem. His bicycle is still running well and there is a good chance that one of the small towns down the road will have a bike shop. He isn't worried. And there is something more important. Kelly. With the mountain wind rattling the canvas of his tent, he happily pulls in a short text from her. It is full of questions and sweet wishes. He answers, describing his meeting with Will Chang and telling her about his plans to stay at Beaver Lake one more day. He doesn't mention his bike problem.

There is nothing from his parents. He sends them a text message telling them where he is. As he composes the message, he notices an interesting change in himself. The issues he had had with them before he left home seem less important. He isn't ready to turn around and go home, but he is finding that his original idea, just to keep going, has become questionable. He finally dozes off thinking that after a few more weeks of riding, he will go home after all … maybe … probably.

Back home in Argyle, Bob and Lynn Mayer sit in their living room discussing their younger son. Ed looks thoughtfully at his wife. "He and his buddy have been gone for nearly a week. I was certainly wrong about them getting discouraged and turning around in just a few days."

Lynn nods, "I think he is more like you than you think, Bob. Persistent – goal oriented. I'm sure he needs this cycling adventure as a break from us – an important growing-up part of his life." Some tears appear in the corners of her eyes. "I just want him to be safe."

Bob walks over to his wife and kneels next to her chair. He puts his hand on her arm and speaks softly. "Lynn, they'll be OK. They have been gone a little more than a week and from Josh's latest text, they are taking a break at some place called Beaver Lake. I checked it out on the net. From the photos and text, it seems like a good place with camping facilities and a store next to a pretty impressive lake. Josh's emails tell me that the toughest part of the trip is over."

Lynn asks, "When will they be back home?"

"If I understood Josh's original plan, I think he and his buddy will turn around in a few more days. They should be home in a week and a half or so."

Bob walks back to his chair and sits quietly. Lynn's tears are back as she broke the silence, "Ed will be off to college by the end of the summer and now Josh is growing up so fast that I hardly recognize him. What ever happened to those little boys we used to carry around?"

15.

Early the next morning, Josh is up early to say goodbye to Will. They exchange email addresses, then Will is on his bike and down the road to the south. Josh is still tired. He walks slowly back to his tent and crawls back into his sleeping bag. The sun's rays begin to filter through the trees, dappling his tent with constantly moving shadows. He falls back to sleep.

Josh finally rolls out of bed about eight-thirty. He is well rested only a few aches from his hard days of riding. The second day at Beaver Lake Camp is one of pure contentment. His supplies have grown with an hour of shopping at the camp store. A bottle of orange juice with fruit and some milk poured over his cold cereal are consumed in record time. He laughs at his so-called biking diet, "Same old food most days, but it's good, it's quick, and it keeps me going!"

After washing his plate, cup, and silverware at a common sink thirty feet from his tent, he decides he needs to do some clothes washing—especially socks and underwear that were, well, "gross!" is what he writes in his diary.

Later, with his clean laundry hanging on a short piece of rope between two trees, he sits in a shady spot and exchanges texts with Kelly. She is really enjoying her bookstore and babysitting jobs.

Her words, "I think about you a lot, Josh," brings her smiling blue eyes to his mind's eye. Josh sits on the ground, his back against a nearby pine tree swaying in the morning breeze. He closes his eyes and thinks about Kelly and their kiss on the day he left.

Josh almost falls asleep again when his thoughts turned to the problem Will Chang had discovered with Josh's bike. Better check it out one more time.

Josh walks over to his bicycle for a short ride. Yes, for the first time, he feels the problem with his rear axle as he pedals slowly around the camp parking lot. It doesn't seem like much, but there's no doubt. Something is wrong.

The question facing him now is what to do? He searches the net for bike shops along his route. Most are a long way from Beaver Lake. The nearest one was is in Silverville, at least two days farther north. Another solution is to going back to a small bike shop that was a little closer. Josh was stubborn. He just isn't ready to go backwards. He decides that Silverville will be his goal. If he pushes it, he can be there sooner. Certainly, the problem should be manageable for a couple of days.

Early the next day, Josh leaves Beaver Lake Camp on the road north. He feels well rested and his bike is rolling smoothly; he is happy to be riding again!

Soon, he is back in the deep forest where the roads are well shaded and dry. He covers a nearly 82 miles in less than six hours of riding time and there was no evidence of any problem with his bike. He's a happy guy!

Looking for a safe spot in the forest to camp for the night, he pedals around the next curve in the road to see a small diner with and a gas station off to one side.

Josh leans his bike against a railing of a small porch and walks up the steps to the diner. Smells of French fries, fried onions, and burgers reminded him how hungry he is. By the time he sits on a stool in and puts his elbows the aging Formica counter to check out the menu, he is definitely ready for a hamburger dinner.

The woman behind the counter is fifty something. She wears a gray uniform with a fading name tag that identifies her as 'Edie.' Black hair with streaks of gray are piled on her head. A small white hat holds it crookedly in place. Her cigarette-roughened voice falls sharply on Josh's ear. "Whadaya want, buster?"

"Oh, hi … a … a … I think I want a hamburger. A burger with fries."

Holding her pencil poised to take his order, she didn't write anything. "Listen, skinny, I don't know who you are, but looking at you, I'd say that a burger and fries won't quite do it. You better have a milkshake—and onion rings. The wind is going to blow you away unless you put some muscle on!"

Josh feels his face reddening. "Oh, OK. OK. I'll have it all."

"Can you afford it?"

Josh pauses, doing a mental check of his cash available.

"Yep, I can."

Taking his order, Edie's rough demeanor began to soften as she assessed Josh from a distance. She was thinking, *Just a kid.*

Ten minutes later, she brings a tray piled high with dishes of food to the counter where Josh sits. "Ok kid, here you go. Be sure to clean your plate!"

Josh is embarrassed to hear what his mother used to say to him when he was a little kid.

Edie gives him a smile when she notices his blush. "Hey, don't take that too personally, it's just that you remind me of my little brother a long time ago." Laughing, she admitted that she also used to give him hell!

Josh relaxes, understanding that Edie is a nice person with just a bit of a rough exterior. Since he is the only customer at the counter, they soon find themselves talking easily about his trip and her job and the surrounding community.

It is almost evening when Josh decides he had better get some sleep for tomorrow's ride. "Hey Edie, thanks for the talk. I've met a lot of people on this ride but I think you have been one of the nicest. If I come back this way, I'll drop by again." Edie reaches across the counter and pats Josh's hand, "You be careful"

He gives her a great smile and waves a friendly good bye when walks out, "I will."

A few minutes later, the gas station operator gives him permission to set up his camp in the nearby woods.

The following morning, after a good night's sleep, Josh rides his bike into the mountain town of McKenzie. The bicycle continues to roll well, despite Will Chang's gloomy prediction. Of course, the big question is, will his luck hold?

McKenzie is typical of many of the small towns he has encountered on his trip. 'Downtown' is a stretch of a description of the place. It amounts to a gas station, auto repair shop, and a parking lot on one side of the road and a few cabins and a combination café-grocery store on the other—a good place for a root beer stop.

When Josh leaned his bike next to the stairs of the café, he notices a group of scruffy-looking teenagers sitting idly on their bicycles watching him from across the street. He mumbles to himself, "I guess I'm not the only ragged-looking cyclist in town."

A few minutes later, with a soda bottle and a candy bar in hand, he walks into the parking lot to find his bike on its side, with the contents of one saddle bag scattered across the ground. Four guys about his age are kicking around his spilled clothes and equipment.

Josh drops his drink, Josh sprints towards them, causing them to scatter. One of them laughs harshly over his shoulder and shouts, "Hey fuck-head bike-rider! You have just been screwed!"

At that moment, a police car pulls into the parking lot. The boys who had been rifling Josh's saddle bags run off as the officer stops his car and gets out. He walks over to Josh. "What's happening, son?"

"I just came out of that café to find those jerks going through my saddle bags." He picks up a dumped saddle bag and grits his teeth angrily; the face of his smart-phone is cracked. "Damn! Have I got a problem!"

The police officer takes down Josh's name and particulars. He is pessimistic about giving any real help. "Sorry kid. If I'd been here just a little sooner, I might have identified those guys—probably locals. But, unfortunately, didn't get a good look at them and you probably don't know them."

Josh gives a resigned head shake and says, "You're right, I don't. Thanks anyway, at least you chased them away."

After the officer drove off, Josh repacks his saddle bags then sits down a curb to check out his phone. He holds it up to his ear, then shakes it. Something is rattling around. What? He wasn't sure. He punched a couple of keys to bring up a favorite website. He is relieved. Tonight, he'll give Kelly a call to see if the phone will work despite the crack and the rattle. A few minutes later, he rides out of town, breathing a little easier over what could have been a real disaster.

16.

An hour or so north of McKenzie, the road Is empty. Josh hasn't seen any vehicles for the last hour or so. The late morning sun is already hot. There are no deer or squirrels to be seen. The place has sort of a dead feeling. A few cries of Blue Jays are the only sounds accompanying the rhythm of his pedaling.

The tall, green trees that walled the road he was riding on just a day earlier are now few and far between. His view is of miles of open slopes covered with low scrub brush and the remains of a forest – charred trees – blackened, stub-like sticks. It is obvious that a large fire had recently burned through this area. It is eerie to be so high in the mountains in an area marked 'forest' on his map and yet have no trees blocking his view. The ravages of the past fire raise an uneasiness in Josh's thoughts. The sooner he can get out of there, the better. He stands up on his pedals to ride up another hill.

Soon he has other things to worry about. A distinct grinding noise in his rear wheel gets his attention. He begins to ride up what should have been an easy climb, but his pace becomes harder and slower. He finally steps off his bike and begins to walk.

Twenty minutes later, he leans his bike against a 5,000-foot elevation sign. He tries to check his location on his smartphone. No reception. His odometer shows him to be only 15 miles north of McKenzie. Not very good for nearly three hours. The steepening road across the burned slope is no fun. Walking, pushing, and pulling his bike uphill is not only slower than riding, but it's awkward and harder.

Tired and very warm, he takes regular swigs of water from his canteen. He opens his pack; when the canteen gives out, there will be only one bottle of water remaining. The situation isn't good. He tries to stay positive, but he knows he will be lucky to squeeze another 10 miles out of his remaining water supply. A crow on a bare, black limb of a burned tree cocks its head as if to warn Josh and caws loudly.

Josh bangs his fist on his bike helmet, "You dummy, this is bad planning. Where have you been?"

He looks up at the smoky sky and speaks to himself a little more quietly, more positively. "OK cyclist, let's do the job right. Drink a little less water and walk a little faster and look for a creek."

The observant crow tilted its head and gave Josh another loud "Caw!" and flew off. Josh laughed at the sound, "That must mean, *Good luck and keep moving, kid!*

A half hour later, the crow's good advice starts to fade with a couple of other issues. Josh starts to feel some rubbing in his bike shoes. With cleats and low heels, they aren't designed for walking very far. Now, he had to stop every ten minutes or so to shake out sand and small rocks.

Finally, he takes a deep breath and says, "What the hell!" He drops his bike on its side and fishes a pair of running shoes out one of his saddle bags. He slips them on and ties the laces. Now he can comfortably wiggle his toes. Standing, with a sigh of relief, his walking quickly improves.

An hour or so later, Josh sits next to his bike and spreads out his new map with its great detail. It looks like there is a 6,100-foot pass ahead. At the rate he is walking, that could take about three hours. After that, he has another 25 miles to the next campground but, the best thing, it'll be downhill!

He is now dealing with a bunch of "maybes." Maybe he can coast down that hill. Maybe not. He has the sinking feeling that he is going to spend another night in the woods. Maybe there'll be some water around. Maybe not.

Ignoring the worry, Josh shrugs his weary shoulders in an effort to loosen them up. He stands, ready to move again. He pushes his bike a little faster up the hill.

Forty minutes later, he is sitting on a large rock on the shoulder of the road, sipping at his dwindling water supply. He doesn't want to think about it, but, despite his running shoes, he is pushing his bike more slowly. He exhales a deep sigh of frustration at the situation. What can he do?

Something positive. He pulls out his smart phone to give Kelly a call – he needs her encouragement. There is only a weak, sporadic connection, if any. They can't even text each other.

Josh looks at the sky. More trouble. The clouds are tall and gray and illuminated by distant flashes of lightning to the north. He gives an ironic laugh, "I just need a <u>little</u> water, not a thunderstorm!"

Weariness is on his mind as he begins pushing his bike again. He can hear the sound of a truck coming up the hill behind him. It is the first vehicle he has seen in more than three hours. The 10-wheeler was in a low gear, climbing noisily up the hill. It passes Josh who is standing well off the road. Then, with a hiss of its brakes, it slows and pulls onto the shoulder.

Josh begins to push his bike around the parked truck in an effort to avoid the dust and diesel smoke. The driver leans out of his window and shouts, "Hey kid! Need a lift?"

Josh can't believe his luck. He yells, "Yes, yes I do!" He pushes his bike up to the truck. The driver gets out, opening some huge loading doors on the side of the vehicle. Josh can see that there is plenty of room for his bike.

Just as they lift his bike and bags aboard and tie them down, the rain begins. Josh couldn't believe his luck. "Thanks a lot, Mr. ..."

"I'm Cal. What's your name?"

"Josh ... make that 'a really tired-of-walking Josh,'" he laughs, and drops into the passenger seat with a great sigh of relief.

Cal, about 40, is a heavy, rugged-looking guy with straight brown hair falling over his ears and forehead, brushing the tops of his sunglasses. An unkempt mustache hangs over the sides of his smiling mouth. He wears a short-sleeved checkered shirt, jeans, and heavy boots.

Josh settles back in his seat and thanks Cal again. "You saved me from the rain. I'm a lucky guy!"

"Glad I can help, Josh. A little company is good for me, too"

Cal expertly moves his big rig back onto the road, handling it with ease. He glances over at his tired-looking, young passenger. "Son, I have a question. This road isn't that steep. In fact, every cyclist I've ever seen along here has been pedaling. I don't get it, you look like you're in good shape, but you're walking. What's the deal? Are you hurt? Is your bike broken?"

"Yeah, it's my bike. I have a problem with my back wheel. It'll turn fairly easily at very slow speeds – walking speeds but, if I try to pedal any faster, it ties up. I don't have the tools to fix it. I think I need a new part – some bearings or something. I know there is a bike shop in Silverville. Are you going that far?" His words came out in a rush.

Cal turns on his wipers as rain increases in intensity. He adjusts expertly to the rapidly changing wet conditions, easily handling the big rig. Josh relaxes, happy to be in a warm, dry cab rather than in the bushes and in the rain, trying to put up his tent.

The trucker glances over at Josh, "I'm afraid I won't be going through Silverville. I have to turn east at Northland, about 40 miles this side of that town. Wish I could help more."

"That's OK, Cal. A rest and ride in a dry truck is just what I need. I can make it to my next campground from your turnoff."

Josh notices that the cab was personalized with what looks like family memorabilia: one photo of a couple of wide-eyed kids and another of a pretty, smiling woman were pinned to the dashboard. A toy bear hangs from the mirror. Cal is a family guy. Josh is comfortable talking with him.

"Cal, when I started out this morning, I was headed for a campground called 'Three Trees.' Do you know it?"

"Yep, I do. I usually stop there for a meal on this route. It seems like a nice place next to a creek. Good fishing. There's even a small beach and wide spot in the creek for swimming. On one of my stops for lunch a couple of weeks ago I ran into the camp supervisor at the restaurant across the road. We had a great talk. Nice guy – he showed me around the campground. Can't remember his name, Lemon or Linton or something like that. He and a couple of other employees, young guys, do a good job running the place."

"Three Trees campground has an office and a small store, some cabins, a lot of campsites, showers, and clean out-houses. You'll like it." Cal glances knowingly at his weary passenger. "You might consider staying a couple of days, just for a rest and a clean-up. We'll be over the hill and down there in about 30 minutes."

Josh makes his decision. "You're right. I'm going to stop there for a day or so while I figure out what I'm to do about my busted bike. Maybe I can catch a ride on another truck to Silverville."

When they arrive opposite the entrance to the campground, it had stopped raining. The afternoon sun is just peeking out of the broken cloud cover when Cal suggests that they grab a bite to eat. Josh realizes that with all the worry about his bike, and having enough water, and finding a place to stay, he hadn't thought much about food. Yep, he is very hungry and very thirsty!

They walk into the brightness and good smells of the restaurant to sit down and enjoy good meals of burgers and fries. Conversation continues to be easy, filled with tales and good laughs about themselves and their travels.

Afterwards, they return to Cal's truck and unload Josh's bike. Cal gives him a firm handshake and steps up into his cab. He smiles down at his young passenger, "Hope you solve your bike problems without too much trouble. Enjoy the rest of your ride, kid. Who knows? Maybe I'll see you out here again. Take it easy!"

Josh waves then watches the truck for a couple of minutes as it rumbles down the road.

17.

B ill Lyndon just steps out of his office to see a slender young guy carrying a cycling helmet unload his bike from a ten-wheeler stopped across the road. Lyndon is the supervisor of Three Trees Campground. At 30 years old and 6'2," he has a rugged outdoor look, dressed in heavy shoes and jeans with red suspenders over his long-sleeved shirt. He pushes his cowboy hat back over his short brown hair and watches Josh push his bike across the road.

He thinks about his own teenage adventures so long ago and his journey to Three Trees. He had enlisted in the Army when he was 18. His service in Iraq had made him grow up—maybe too fast. When his enlistment was up, he had gone to junior college with a concentration in business. He was good with numbers and decided to be a bookkeeper—steady work and decent pay. He had no trouble landing a good job when his studies were completed. But there was a hiccup in his plan. He soon discovered that he wasn't ready to process numbers eight hours a day. Solitary hours spent sitting at a computer wore on him. He wanted more contact with people. Management came to mind. Especially with his army experience, he knew he had the maturity and experience to super-vise people. His officers had told him that with his smarts and per-sonality, he was a natural leader.

While overseeing people on a job might have been one of his strengths, managing his personal life is sometimes a challenge. He never married, although he came close a couple of times. His war experiences had left him too antsy for a permanent relationship.

Bill bounced from job to job until he finally discovered the quiet and refreshing environment of the California Forests. Initially, he found a job managing a motel near the town of Mt. Shasta. Then, this past spring, the opportunity to manage Three Trees Campground came up. He took it. It was a great decision. He loves the job. Even though he knows it is just a summer proposition, he can make good contacts for later employment in the Forest Service.

His management sense is working as he watches the young fellow wheel his bike through the entrance to Three Trees. Bill has a feeling that this kid may be able help him solve a personnel problem that had just come up. He will certainly talk to him.

With a wave at the Cal's departing truck, Josh pushes his bike across the road to check out the camp where he will spend the night. A large sign identifying "Three Trees Campground" stretches above the entrance to a wide parking lot surrounded by a thick forest. On one side of the parking lot is a wood frame building—a combination camp office and camp store. Back among the trees, cabins and a few tents dot the property. In the distance, the pines give way to patches of manzanita along a creek with patchy white beaches. Josh leans on his bike for a minute, taking in the pleasant surroundings. The hassle of walking and pushing his bike over so many miles of hills seems less important now. His first priorities now are food and a good sleep. Tomorrow, he'll run to the white beach a jump in that cold creek.

Josh drops his bike on the edge of the parking lot and steps up to the office to register. Bill Lyndon is standing on the porch watching the young cyclist. He greets Josh, "Welcome to Three Trees, cyclist! I'm Bill Lyndon, the Camp Director. When you get settled, I'd like to talk to you about your bike trip. Looks like you have been on the road for a while."

Josh laughed, pulling on his bike shirt and wrinkling his nose. "Ugh! Both my clothes and I need a good washing! Let me get cleaned up, then I'll tell you about my crazy trip"

Bill points to the doorway, "You can talk to Jose' inside. He'll get you registered."

They part with a handshake. Josh leans his bike on a convenient pine tree and walks into the park office. The registration desk is manned by a well-tanned, dark-haired fellow probably about 18 or 19. His name tag reads "Jose Serrano." About 5'10" and 180lbs, Jose' is obviously in excellent shape. He looks up at Josh with a smile, "Welcome to Three Trees, my friend. What can I do for you?"

"I need a spot to stay for a night or two or three. I'm not exactly sure. I think all that I really need is a campsite. He points over his shoulder to his bike in the parking lot, "I'm on a long trip and I have some mechanical problems to fix before I can move on.

"All of my gear is on my bike. I just a need a spot a to pitch a tent."

Jose' is impressed. "A bike! Wow! Where did you come from?"

Josh gave Jose' a short description of his trip from Argyle, along the mountains, then finally to Three Trees. He explains, "I have been pedaling –," he shook his head with a grin — "make that pedaling <u>and</u> walking – for **XX** days!" He laughs, "Both my bike and I need a rest!

"Where are you from, Jose'?"

"Mission City, just east of L.A. Not five miles from Argyle. Now that's something! Even though we live only a few miles apart, we meet for the first time 300 miles away in the middle of the forest!"

Josh and Jose' share some stories about their homes and families. Jose' has two brothers and two sisters, all younger. Although their school teams are in different leagues, they had played many preseason baseball, basketball, and football games.

Josh asks, "Did you play any sports, Jose?"

"I did. A lot of baseball and track and field. I ran the mile and two-mile. I just didn't click in football. And basketball wasn't my game. I was too short, and playing indoors just didn't cut it for me. I'm an outdoor guy," He laughs, "That's why I'm here! How about you?"

Josh chuckles, "As far as high school sports are concerned, you'd call me a spectator. My main sport is cycling." Josh grins, standing up a little taller. "And I think I'm getting better at it."

Jose' describes some of his cycling experiences. "I liked it but, after I was about 12, I gave up my bike. None of my buddies did it. Just too much traffic where we lived."

Josh agreed, "Even though my home town is on the edge of L.A., we still have to fight through some serious traffic at the start of our rides. Luckily, there are some great trips once you get out and onto the side roads in the hills and away from those crazy downtown drivers.

Josh was curious about this guy who was only a few years older than he was. "How did you come by this job, Jose'?"

"I had always been interested in forestry, but I didn't know much about it. After I graduated from high school last month, I thought a couple of months in the woods might help me figure out if I liked it. I'm too young and not really trained for a job in the Forest Service, so when I saw this summer job advertised on the net, I jumped on it."

Their relaxed conversation lasts a few more minutes, then Josh registers and pays the camping fee. Jose' shows him a map of the camp and recommends the best sites. "You want something far enough from the water so the mosquitoes don't make you crazy, and close enough to the toilets and showers so you won't have to walk a quarter mile just to pee or shower. Number 20 is a good one and it's open. In fact, you don't have any neighbors within 50 yards. Nice and quiet!"

Jose' walks over from the registration desk to the counter at the camp store and waits while Josh picks up a can of beans, a loaf of bread, crackers and a root beer. There are some oranges and grapes available and he grabs a couple of bags of those. With thanks and a friendly wave to Jose', he leaves the camp store and pushes his bike along one of the access roads. A few minutes later, he is at his campsite. Jose' was exactly right: it is quiet with good access to restrooms and showers.

Josh sets up his camp in record time. A little later, he enjoys a fantastic shower, washing away a few days of dirt. He even takes advantage of the sink to deal with some grimy underwear, T-shirts, and socks. Back at his camp, he stretches a nylon cord between two small trees to dry his clean clothes. Then, as usual, he hangs his food from a nearby tree, out of the reach of those pesky night critters.

Ever curious, Josh takes a walk around the campground. Beyond Three Trees, he can see heavily forested hillsides that give way to high mountain peaks clearly above the tree line. There is still a late June smattering of snow under steep cliffs. The view is astoundingly beautiful and quietly calming. He needs that.

He sits on a convenient boulder just outside his tent and calls his parents—no voice contact. He finally gets through with a brief text:

AM OK HAVIN FUN AT 3 TREES CAMP WILL CALL/TXT IN AM JOSH

Then Kelly. Voice contact is poor. A few of her words came a few minutes later by text message: "MISS YOU" and "WHERE ARE YOU?" He manages to get one text message through, "I'M OK. TAKING A REST FOR A 2 DAYS WILL TRY TO CALL TOMORROW"

He puts his smart-phone away and stretches out in his sleeping bag. He'll use his flashlight to study his map and then write some notes in his journal. Before he can unfold the map, he's asleep.

An early breakfast starts Josh's next morning. After that, his priority is to repair his bike. He removes the rear wheel to see if he can figure out a fix. It is soon clear that he isn't going to get very far. He needs some help.

Maybe, he can catch a ride on a truck going into Silverville. That would take a lot of hanging around the restaurant across the street to convince some truck driver to give him a ride and to bring his broken bike along. He needs a plan— he needs some time to think.

He sits down on a soft patch of pine needles with his elbows on his knees and his head in his hands. His frustrations grow when he considered his limited options. He still wants to ride, but now he couldn't even turnaround and ride back home.

He is suddenly brought out of his gray mood when the sound of a friendly voice falls on his ears. "Hi kid, how's it going?"

It's Bill Lyndon, the campground director. He checks out Josh's newly constructed campsite and nods his approval, adding, "Your camp setup sure looks like you know what you're doing."

Josh stands and shakes hands with his visitor. "Thanks Bill. This is a great place for my tent. Jose' has been a big help."

He stretches his arms and gives a relaxed smile, "I had a fantastic shower and found some clean clothes in my saddle bags. I'm good!"

But then he pauses, puts his hands on his hips, and says hesitantly, "Well … actually … I'm not so good.

"I'm glad you came by. I was going to ask you for some advice on the route for the next part of my ride." He shakes his head and smiles ironically, "But that has all changed. I'm afraid my bike is done with me!"

With his arms crossed, Bill leans over Josh's bicycle. "What's the problem?"

Josh describes the dragging on his back wheel. He asks Bill if he has any experience with bike repair.

Bill shakes his head with an apologetic frown, "Aside from knowing how to fix an occasional flat, your problem is way outside my 'fix-it' ability, Josh. I don't think I can help."

Josh stands and brushes some pine needles off of his board shorts. "Since my bike problem first developed, my plan has been to pedal to a bike shop in Silverville. Now things have obviously changed. The dragging is so bad I can't even ride. Unless I find someone to haul my bike and me up to Silverville, I'm done."

Josh is at a low point, "I think I'm going to be looking for a bus ride home."

Bill rubs his chin thoughtfully. He glances at the treetops for a moment. You are right, Josh. "We don't get any trucks stopping here regularly. A rig like the one that brought you here is not usual—maybe a couple of times a week, if that."

He can see the disappointment growing on Josh's face. "OK kid, here's one possibility. There are two weekly buses that travel north through here to Silverville. One was here yesterday and there'll be another on Sunday.

"It's not unusual for them to be packed with passengers and their luggage, so I can't guarantee they'll have room for your bike, but if they do, you'll make to Silverville and your bike shop."

Bill shrugs his shoulders, "With no other ways to go, it's worth a try."

Josh tries to be upbeat about Bill's solution. "I'm not too worried about getting my bike aboard a bus. I can break it down into a fairly small package. But what I don't know is whether or not the problem is fixable. And, if it is, how long will it take? I have some money, but the bus ride, plus at least one overnight in Silverville and the cost of the repair will certainly stretch my—he laughed—my so-called budget. It'll be tight. I guess I have a lot to think about in the few days before that next bus arrives."

Bill asks the same questions that Josh has answered many times over the last two weeks. Where was he from? How long had he been on the road? Josh was comfortable and clear in answering most of them.

Josh attempted to change the subject before Bill started asking about his age. He asked Bill an unrelated question about Three Trees. "Bill, most of the campgrounds I have seen of this size are managed by either the California Forestry Service or USFS. But the truck driver who gave me my last lift said that this one is different. Why?"

Bill is quick to answer. "This site does belong to USFS, but it has only recently come over to them from a private owner. But, right now, they don't have the people to manage it. They hired me to work under contract to run Three Trees Campground for this summer."

Josh leans over his bike and turns the pedals for what is probably the tenth time, hoping he not to hear the grinding sound that still falls on his ears. He tries to change the subject, saying to Bill, "I probably haven't been here long enough to see your whole team, but only people I see working here are you and Jose.' Are their others?"

"No, I'm afraid the only people running this place right now are Jose' and me. Last week, we just lost the third member of our team. He had some family problems."

Bill sizes up Josh. He had struck a chord for the Three Trees manager. He needs another worker right now. He looks healthy enough and certainly seems responsible; however, he does look young.

Bill Lyndon stands silently for a few seconds. He seems to be inspecting the limbs of a nearby pine tree. He repeats himself, "Yeah, it's just Jose' and me."

He makes his decision. "Josh, I have a solution for you. Not quite what you are thinking about, but something to consider. Can you help me out here at Three Trees for a few weeks?"

Josh stands up, holding onto his bike, "I don't understand. Help you out? How?"

"Since we lost the other guy, it has been a little tough for two of us to keep the place in shape. I need some help. I'm looking for someone who I can depend on to work for me for five weeks or so and I need him now."

Josh looks up at Bill, frowning curiously. "Me? Are you thinking of me?"

"Yep, I am. You are on the young side, but a guy who can ride a bike to the places you have is smart enough to learn the job and tough enough to hang in there when things are busy.

"Look at it this way. Rather than searching for a bike shop trying to solve your sticky bike problem, consider this other possibility where you won't have to ride – make that— try to ride. Instead, I'm offering you a chance to put that bike away and go to work with Jose' and me.

Josh is certainly interested but, at the same time, he is hesitant to jump into something he knows so little about. "Exactly what would I do?"

"Your job would be camp ground maintenance, cleaning up and repairing the cabins, keeping the grounds and outhouses clean, and occasionally working in the camp store. Most weeks you would work six days. Some of the time we will be up late or working on a day off to fix something that some dumb camper has screwed up. When business is slow, we kick back. I have to tell you, July 4th is coming up in a few days and we will be into the high season. After that, I doubt that there will be much 'kicking back' until sometime in August, maybe later.

"So, there you go. I'm offering you four or five weeks of work. Interested?"

"What would I make?" Bill gave him a number that was more than he made at Mr. Steeler's shop. "You will work six days a week, meals and lodging are included. Interested?"

Josh is more than interested. A job? Room? Board? Working in this beautiful place? How can he turn it down? Doing something else besides riding is just what he needs. His sore butt has been in the saddle for a lot of days and not worrying about fixing his bike would be a relief. Of course, making some money would be terrific! He tries to control his growing enthusiasm as Bill goes on.

"This camp is usually open through mid-August, depending on the tourist traffic. If you are as good as I think you are, you can stay on through end of the season. The only problem would be if my supervisors decide to close the place early. At worst, you can plan on four weeks work. Probably more than that.

Josh doesn't hesitate, "When do I start?"

Bill has a smile of relief on his face, "Great! You begin tomorrow morning!"

He reaches out to shake Josh's hand and adds, "I should warn you that, by taking on this job, you are committing to do a lot work. With only three of us running the place, everybody has to contribute their share.

"Walk with me and I'll show you around.

"Today, you can move your gear into one of our cabins." Bill points to a structure about 30 yards away. "You'll be sharing that tent-cabin with Jose, the guy you met in the office. He's a little older than you and he knows how this place works—a good source of information. And he's a nice guy. You'll like him."

Bill and Josh walk up to an empty tent cabin. Bill explains, "As you can see, the walls and roof are made up of a wood frame covered in canvas. There are two bunks, with mattresses, sheets, towels and blankets provided. You both have a locker inside to store your personal items. You can probably put your bike out of the way under the raised wooden floor of the cabin.

He points to a water faucet in front of the cabin and the nearby locations of showers and outhouses. I have to warn you, these tent-cabins and much of the other equipment in the camp are old. It's up to you to keep them clean and in useable shape.

A few minutes later Bill and Josh stand in the kitchen in one corner of the camp office building. Bill points at a large refrigerator, "You have a couple of choices for meals. For breakfast, there is always milk, juice, fresh fruit, and cold cereal. If you get up early enough, we have a waffle-maker and a frying pan for eggs and bacon. The refrigerator will be well-stocked; I take care of that and all other supplies. You can be sure that you won't go hungry. Lunch and evening meals will vary, depending on how busy we are outside and who is cooking. Can you cook, Josh?"

Josh laughed, shaking his head." I think I'll be the permanent dishwashing guy. Aside from cold cereal for breakfast, a peanut butter sandwich for lunch, and more sandwiches for dinner, my cooking talents are zilch."

Bill smiled at Josh's honest response. "Well Josh, until you learn to cook – and you will – you inherit the responsibility for keeping the kitchen clean. It MUST be cleaned after every meal. That includes clearing the table and washing and drying the dishes and pots and pans and putting them away. Jose' knows all about these jobs. If you have any questions, just ask him."

Josh took a deep breath, thinking that he had better have a good talk with Jose'. He asks Bill what time he starts in the morning. "Breakfast prep at 5:45am, breakfast served at 6:30am, Camp work usually starts about seven."

Josh is almost speechless when he considers this new and way different opportunity that has suddenly been dropped in lap—meals, a cabin, and really interesting work—and no biking! He wants to jump up and down and yell. He enthusiastically shakes hands with Bill, "Wow! I'll be ready! Thanks a lot!"

Josh considers his good luck on his walk back to his campsite. This chance to work and make some money is almost unbelievable. The rest of his summer schedule is set. Would he miss biking? What about that **600**-mile goal that he and Ron had talked about last spring? He has something like **450** miles under his belt so far. That is more than he has ever done in a single trip. In fact, it is more than he's done in a whole summer. Nah, he isn't disappointed. He's stoked about this new and unexpected job opportunity in the wilderness. This'll be his best summer – ever!

Back in his tent, he pulls out his cycling diary. This will be his last entry for quite a while. Skimming through the pages, they are mostly filled with distances for each day and a few lines about plans for the next day. On a couple of stops he had been too tired to write anything except mileage. He shook his head at the daily numbers, they certainly reflected the terrain— some 30-mile days and some 60-mile days. More interesting were the hours he was in the saddle. His shortest day was four hours and his longest was 13. Whether he does any more riding or not, he had set his own personal record.

But now he was, in bicycle jargon, 'changing gears'—starting a new adventure at Camp Three Trees. He wonders what his family would think about where he is and what he is doing? What will Kelly think? He'll call them.

18.

Josh steps out of his tent the next morning to watch the rising sun gradually illuminate the campground. He is ready and excited to get started with his new job at the Camp Three Trees. He folds up his tent and hauls his gear to the cabin he'll be sharing with Jose' Serrano.

Twenty minutes later, his saddle bags and their contents are stored in a footlocker and his bed is made—a real bed with clean sheets, blankets and a pillow. He plops down on it. An early nap is tempting, but he has too much to do.

Josh steps outside to break down his bike for storage. He pauses for a few seconds to look over the two-wheeler that has brought him so far. He shakes his head, patting the handlebars, "You've done a good job, old bicycle. But, now, it's time for a rest."

He removes the wheels and rack to make a more compact package that he wraps it a couple of garbage bags. He ties it up with a piece of rope and to store it under his tent-cabin. For a moment, he has mixed feelings about his bike trip being over. But that regret is quickly replaced by his excitement about his new job at Camp Three Trees.

Josh is about to run over to the kitchen to get a little breakfast when Jose' walks up. Standing in the doorway of their cabin with his arms crossed and a stern look, Jose' checks out Josh's efforts to set up their tent.

A smile creeps across his face and then he breaks up with laughter. "I was going to give you hell for screwing up this place when you moved all your stuff in—but, you know, I think you've got it! Way to go, newbie, you can stay!"

Josh gives Jose' a deep bow, "My pleasure, oh great fellow worker."

They both laugh at his antics, then shake hands and talk for a while. Finally, Josh excuses himself, waving his smart phone, "Got to call home and let them know I'm still alive!"

He sits on the steps outside his tent and calls Kelly. She answers on the first ring.

"Hey Kelly, It's me, the wayward cyclist! Missing you a lot! "

She giggles, "Hi Josh! I bet I miss you more!"

"Nah, impossible. I miss you sooo much I could—explode!"

They laugh at their words, both very happy to be sharing a few minutes together, even if it is only on their smart-phones.

Josh asks Kelly about her summer in Argyle. She replies, "Busy! I'm now working 12 hours a week at the bookstore and I have picked up three more baby-sitting jobs.

"The bookstore is so interesting! I have learned how to use the cash register and now I can even talk to customers about electronic books. It is great fun. I meet a lot of people. And when I have some free time, I have been taking my youngest brother, Billy, to the swimming pool a couple of times a week. He has just finished swimming lessons and is now a little fish!"

They talk and laugh about Kelly's adventures at home. Then Kelly asks about his bike ride. "How far did you ride yesterday? Where are you now?

Josh describes his change in plans. "Kelly, I am up here at a place called Three Trees Campground. I've had a problem with my bike. It's broken. I can't fix it and the nearest bike shop is miles away. So I am off my bike. That's a bad deal."

Kelly answered in worried tones, "Josh! Your bike is broken? That's terrible! What are you going to do?"

Josh leans back on the steps. He is more relaxed than he has been in a long time. He's very happy with his new opportunity and, best of all, he's now sharing his experience with Kelly.

"Kelly, you won't believe this! Just a couple hours after I had to quit riding because my bike was broken, I was offered a full-time job at a really neat place called Three Trees Campground. Isn't that wild? Turns out that one of their employees had suddenly quit. They offered me the job and I grabbed it. I start work tomorrow morning!

"I have a cabin and meals and the pay is good. I like the guys I'll be working with. There is plenty to do—the place will sure keep me hopping." As he speaks, he sits up and sweeps his hand around a horizon dotted with big trees and framed by tall mountains. "Best of all, I am up here in the High Sierra. It's beautiful country."

"What will you be doing, Josh? And when will I see you?"

Josh hears a catch in her voice and imagines a tear on her freckled cheek. "Ah, Kelly, don't worry. The job will only last until mid-August. I'll be back before you know it! And the phone reception is great up here. We'll be able to talk every day.

"While I'm here, I will be doing a lot of janitor work – cleaning cabins, emptying trash, raking pine needles off the paths, washing dishes. I will even work camper registration now and then. There are only three of us including the boss so we have to do everything.

Kelly could sense Josh' excitement. He went on, waving his hand and pointing to various locations around the camp. "Although no more biking, I will have enough time off to hike and swim and fish. It's a good situation.

"Kelly, one thing that is for sure is that when I am done here, I will put my bike and the rest of my gear on a bus and come straight back to you."

"I think about you all the time. I dream about you—I love you." He whispers the words that were as new to him as his feelings.

The connection is quiet, causing Josh to shake his phone, thinking he had lost contact. She is still there. "Oh Josh, I wish you were coming back sooner. Please be careful."

When their call was over, they both sat miles apart, looking at their phones, wishing they could touch hands.

Josh spends the rest of the day walking around the camp, familiarizing himself with the area, including various paths to the creek the location of tools. He listens to Jose's descriptions of "… important things …," such as the location of the tool shed and the toilet paper supply.

He checks out the kitchen at lunch and, even though his work doesn't start until the next day, he washes the dishes, he walks the boundaries of the camp, and locates the fishing supplies. He is happier with his new job at every turn. The next few weeks are going to be great!

That evening, Josh sits on a bench in front of a deserted camp office to call his parents to tell them where he is, what he is doing; and how much longer he'd be away. He spends a few minutes rehearsing his story then punches in the number on his cell phone. His dad answers. There was a touch of impatience in his voice, "Josh! Where in the heck are you? We haven't heard a thing from you for two days!"

"Sorry Dad, contact is not great up here in the mountains. I want to let you know that there have been a couple of changes in my plans. I'm in the Northern Sierra at a place called Three Trees Campground. You can check out the location on-line."

Josh takes a deep breath before he tells his dad the next part. "My buddy, Ron, isn't with me. He has to be home because his mother is sick."

That story isn't really a lie, but, of course, there is what Josh didn't say. His buddy had NEVER been with him. Thankfully, his dad wasn't aware of that omission. But he was still a little impatient, wanting more information, "What are you going to do now?"

"Well, first of all, I'm off my bike. It's broken and I can't repair it and there are no bike shops around here where I can get some help. So, I've taken a job at this campground and …"

Bob interrupts, "Wait—wait! This is a heck of change. Run that by me again."

Josh reviews his bike problem, then describes his new job, his pay, where he is staying, and about how long he'll be at Three

Trees before returning home. "When I'm done here, I'll pack up my busted bike and the rest of my gear and hop a bus home."

His dad sounds relieved, "That's a good decision, son. But when will we actually see you?"

"Not exactly sure. This camp closes sometime between the 15th and the 30th of August, depending on the tourist activity. I've told them that I have to be on the road by the 20th at the latest because school will be starting up. When I know our schedule better, I'll let you know."

Bob Mayer picked up on his son's confident attitude, realizing that Josh is no longer a kid. He is suddenly a young man capable of making some good decisions.

This was the first time Josh felt that his father wasn't talking 'to him' – he was talking 'with him.' They chat for a bit longer, then his dad hands his phone over to his wife.

Lynn wants to know if Josh was taking care of himself. "Are you washing your clothes regularly?"

Josh chuckles to himself over the 'regularly' part of her question. He tells her, "Mom, I actually washed my clothes this afternoon!"

"And, Mom, there is one other thing. Since I'm working up here, I'm going to need some boots. All I've got beside my bike shoes are some light running shoes and they are too light for the work I'll be doing. If you dig around my room, you'll find my old hiking boots—probably in the back of my closet. It would be great if you could pack them up and send them to me."

"Of course. Give me an address and they'll be in the mail tomorrow."

Josh said, "I haven't got it in front of me. I will dig it out and text it to you, OK?"

"That's fine, son. Now you be careful up there and please call regularly! Here's Dad."

Josh gives a quick description of his work to Bob and then asks many questions about his brother. "What does Ed think about his visit to The University of Colorado? When does he leave to start school? Tell him 'hi' for me."

After the call was over, back home, Josh's parents sit in the living room talking about the adventures of their second son. Bob leans back in his chair, looking at his wife. "You know, Lynn, Josh sounded different. Maybe it was just the connection, but his voice seemed deeper. And another thing, he didn't hesitate to answer questions and explain things to us quite clearly. He suddenly seems older."

Lynn had the same impression. "Yes, older and more responsible. Hmm. His brother was always out in front, in charge, being the best. Josh has always seemed so shy and unsure, hesitating, thinking almost too carefully about what he wants to do next." She looks at her husband, "Maybe we just haven't been paying enough attention."

19.

Jose' shakes Josh's bunk, "C'mon Josh, you're working now. If you want breakfast before we start, you'd better get up and get dressed!"

Josh opens his eyes to see a grinning face. "What? What is going on?"

Jose' laughs at his sleepy cabin-mate. "You are here at Three Trees. You just signed on for a great job doing dishes, sweeping floors, emptying trash, and a lot more of that good stuff. You better get up and enjoy it!"

Josh sits up and rubs his shaggy blond hair. "Oh yeah, Three trees. Sorry Jose', I didn't know where I was for a second. Hang on and I'll walk over to the kitchen with you."

Jose' waits patiently, leaning against the door of the tent cabin with his arms crossed. He smiles at his young co-worker gets ready for his first day at work. Josh throws on an old pair of cutoff blue jeans, a red T-shirt, and his running shoes. He steps outside with a water bottle to brush his teeth and pour the remainder of the water over his head. He towels off and, with a nod to neatness, runs a comb through his fuzzy mop of hair. "OK, I'm ready! Thanks for waiting!"

Jose' gazes with a head shake at Josh's hair, still standing wildly, despite the comb. "Josh, my friend, I think you need a haircut. If you aren't picky, I volunteer."

Josh runs his fingers through his wild blondness. "You cut hair? You really think I need it? Let me think about it."

They walk across the campground. It is already warm, heading for a hot, early July day. Once in the kitchen, Jose' quickly and expertly puts together a great meal of fried eggs, cereal, milk, toast, and fruit—all they can eat. It is the best breakfast Josh has had since he started his bike trip.

A few minutes later, their boss walks in. While he makes his own breakfast, he glances over at Josh. "Okay, Mr. new guy, it starts today. When you finish your breakfast, kitchen clean-up is your chore. We don't have a dish-washing machine, so you're it. Clean off the tables; wash the plates, glasses, silverware, and any pots and pans our meal generates. Put the garbage in the bag in that can over there. When the can is full, take it outside and throw it in the dumpster. Got It?"

Josh nodded, "I've got it!"

"Let's see, its 7AM now. When you are done with this kitchen stuff, say in a half hour, meet me in the office in and I'll lay out the rest of your day."

By the afternoon, Josh had done the breakfast and lunch dishes, dumped the trash; cleaned out a couple of campsites after some visitors had left; cleaned two outhouses and replaced supplies; and raked a long walk between cabins. His learning curve is steep. He finds himself walking back and forth quite a few times to ask Bill or Jose' how to deal with various problems or simply, "What's next?"

At dinner, Bill looks across the table at his new employee, "You surprise me, Josh! For all the running around you did today you don't look very tired. I'd think that by now you'd be ready for bed!"

Josh laughs, "All those days on my bike, especially riding up and down those mountains got me into pretty good shape. I'm glad to be doing something that helps you and Jose'."

Jose' kids him, "Be careful, Josh, Bill is just easing you into this job. You'd think the better you are, the more down time you'll have. Not so; the better you get at it, the more you get to do!"

Bill smiles saying, "I can't argue with that. Fourth of July just a day away. That marks the start of the high season at Three Trees.

After that, more and more visitors will pour in." And that's what happened.

In the next few days, work increases noticeably to match the greater population of campers. Bill watches Jose' and Josh deal with the influx. Not only do they enjoy meeting the campers and helping them get settled, but, from the start, they display a good team ability to anticipate and solve problems.

Days off and long evenings often find Josh and Jose' swimming in a wide, slow-moving portion of the creek just down the hill from the campground. The water is cool, crystal clear, and deep.

They also fish, with the more experienced Jose' showing Josh places where the trout like to hang out. Bill joins them on a few occasions. He is the most successful fisherman of the three, but Jose' is the best cook when it comes to frying the fish for dinner. Jose' explains his talent, "With three brothers and two sisters, if you wanted to eat, you had better learn to cook. My mom taught us all—and Dad, too. In fact, I think Pop was the best cook of all of us."

Josh quickly learns to answer the many questions visitors ask while he keeps up with his chores in the days that follow. He becomes more efficient at his work, getting in even better shape. His legs had always been ripped from cycling, but now his upper body is getting stronger—a result of cutting thick brush, chopping wood, and lifting heavy loads.

Another change he notices is that in his calls home, his parents seem to be a little more interested in his work. He thinks that it is probably that he isn't riding anymore and he now had what his dad would probably call, a real job.

Kelly is another matter. She asks Josh every possible question about his job, his co-workers, the campers, and the place. A typical question is, "What are you and Jose' doing today?" Of course, Josh is happy with her interest. He only wishes his parents were as curious.

Kelly is excited about her own summer work as well, describing experiences at the bookstore and with the kids she babysits.

Lately Josh has noticed that it isn't unusual to have their cell-phone conversations rolling along nicely, when, all at once, Kelly stops talking for a few seconds, as if she is trying to get her words together. Josh always smiles at those moments because he knows what's coming next.

"Joshua, I love you."

"Kelly, you make me want to climb through this phone and hug you and—kiss you!"

More quietness follows Josh's outburst.

Finally, he tells her, "I'll be home in a few weeks, no later than the 22nd of August."

A short while later, after they had said their sweet goodbyes, they both stare at their quiet phones. Thinking.

The days and weeks at Camp Three Trees fly by. The camp is a peaceful place—the sounds of the wind in the pristine forest, the clear bubbling water in the creek, the views of the surrounding mountains topped by beautiful skies. They all have a calming effect on Josh, in fact, on everybody. The campers are happy to be there, a place where vacation means something.

20.

Three busy weeks later, Josh and Jose' are in the kitchen preparing breakfast. It's a hot, late July morning. Jose', in the middle of frying eggs, wrinkles his nose and waves his hand across his face, "I know I'm not the greatest cook, but that smoke I smell isn't from my breakfast. It must be that fire out east."

In the last week, a fire had broken out about 20 miles southeast of Three Trees. Yesterday, all reports had indicated that it was well under control, although a few smoke plumes could be seen in the distance. Visibility at the campground has been unaffected – until now.

They both step onto the porch. In the hazy distance they can see many more white smoke columns reddened by the rising sun.

Jose' squints at the sight. "Something sure is burning out there. This east wind is a bad direction. Coming down the slopes, it'll be hot and dry. That'll stoke the fire and push it our way." He shakes his head, "Not good."

"Have you ever done any fire-fighting?" Josh asks.

"No, but I have talked to a few buddies who fought some brush fires in the foothills east of L.A. They said it was hard, dirty work—sometimes dangerous as hell."

In the next hour, a couple of carloads of new campers arrive at the camp office. By the time Jose' and Josh finish checking them in and showing them their assigned campsites, it is obvious that they are starting to have concerns about the increasing smokiness.

Jose' explained to them, "The smoke is from a fire ten miles or so east of here. We are in regular contact with the Forest Service and they have not issued any warning for us other than a notice for what you can see – smoke and occasionally low visibilities."

The visitors begin to unload sleeping bags, tents, and other equipment. It wasn't long before they were back at the office asking for more information about the fire. With the decreasing visibility and increasing acrid smell of smoke, they are having second thoughts. Jose' shows them a printout of the latest report from the Forest Service. The projections hadn't changed. In the Camp Three Trees area, there is no fire alert, but the smoky conditions are expected to continue for a day or so.

The would-be campers stand outside the office next to their loaded vehicles. They step aside to allow two other carloads of campers leave the campground. After a little more discussion, they decide to do the same. They had never unpacked their gear.

The "Three Trees Three," as Bill, Jose, and Josh now referred to themselves, stand at the entrance of the eerily quiet campground watching the last camper-van disappear down the road. Bill observed, "Well, there go all our customers for a while. Gives us a chance to relax, if you can stand the smoke. With any luck, these conditions will clear up."

Soon they discover that "clearing up" is not the case. The view of the wooded hills surrounding Three Trees became even more limited with the encroaching smoke.

Bill brings Josh and Jose' into the camp office to discuss the situation. He asked the two younger men to take a seat, saying, "We have to discuss this problem that you can see is getting worse."

Tapping the desk with his pencil, Bill has a grim look on his face. "I have been on the phone to the Forest Service. Those campers who left a few hours ago are fortunate to have gotten away when they did. The roads are going to get crowded. A warning has now been issued for all campers to leave the area.

"The gusty east winds are heating us up and drying things out. I've been told that fire is still about eight miles from here. Unfortunately, in the last two hours, it has started moving quickly this way. Two key access roads have already been cut.

Bill pauses to carefully consider his next words. He looks at the two young men in front of him, hoping that they would understand the critical importance of what he was about to say. "The Forest Service is having a problem getting enough personnel and equipment on the fire lines. It's a matter of too many spot fires breaking out and poor access. They need our help."

Jose' frowns, "Doing what?"

"With its facilities, this area will become a key staging area for fighting the fire, especially with its access to the creek. Aside from the water source, our large parking lot can be used as a helicopter landing area to pick up men and equipment and take them the fire lines. There is a problem. They can't get people in here until tomorrow morning. They want us to hold Camp Three Trees until then."

Jose' and Josh look at each other and then over Bill's shoulder at the growing smoke plumes in the distance. Shaking his head, Josh is skeptical, "Hold the campground? Three of us? What can three of us do?"

Bill answered quickly, "Actually, there is a lot. They want us to open up the parking lot to make it easier for helicopters to get in and out and to reduce the fire danger for the buildings here. I don't want to kid you, it won't be easy. We have to take down a lot of trees on the periphery of the parking lot and clear out the brush near the buildings."

Responses from Josh and Jose' were wide-eyed silence.

Jose' then asked quietly, "Do we have another choice?"

With his hands on his hips, Bill looks up, as if inspecting a light fixture on the ceiling. Then he looks back at his two assistants. "The real question is do we try to do something that might help? Or do we cut and run?"

After a few seconds of thought, Jose' shrugs his shoulders, "I don't know what else I'd do or where I'd go. Hell, I'll stay."

Josh doesn't hesitate, "I'm with Jose.' Where do we start?"

Bill was clear, "We start now! Each of us immediately digging a shelter—a 'safe area' for ourselves—in case the fire blows through and we can't get out. He points to a wall map of the Three

Trees Campground. "Here's good spot. It's close to the water and well away from trees and brush. Let's check it out when we get through here.

"We will also have some protective gear, including fire shelters and smoke masks, courtesy of USFS. Some of their people will bring that stuff in by chopper early tomorrow. They'll give us instructions on the use of the equipment. Pay close attention, they'll only have time to go over it once."

Bill, Jose' and Josh walk out of the office and grabbed saws, axes, shovels and rakes from the shed. They turn their attention to the construction of their safe area. First, they dig holes near the creek where they can hunker down if things get bad. Next, they spend an hour widening the path to the creek by cutting down nearby brush and trees and dragging the slash to the other side of the muddy marsh.

A few hours later, the formerly well-shaded parking lot has taken on a wide-open appearance. The Three Trees three are sweating profusely. Jose' laughs at the situation. "Hey Josh, baby, doesn't this make you anxious to get back into your gardening work when you get out of this place? Nothing like mowing and trimming! Won't that be fun?"

Josh laughs with Jose' at the situation. "When I finish with this place, it'll be a long, long time before I want to do any more yard work!"

Bill deals with communications with the Forest Service while Jose' and Josh kept up their cutting and hauling. By about 3p.m., smoky conditions worsen. Nearby mountain slopes are only dim shadows.

Bill's two assistants really don't have the tools they need for such a big job, only a few hand saws and axes and a single chain saw. More importantly, they don't have their smoke masks yet, only damp kerchiefs over their noses and mouths.

In an odd coincidence, much of the Three Trees Camp area had been burned over about 10 years or so ago. Most of the trees they have to cut down are relatively young Jack Pines, a foot in diameter at the most. Bill and his assistants feel fortunate that they aren't working in the forest a few hundred yards away where the older trees are two or three feet thick.

A chainsaw is new for Josh, so Jose' and Bill take turns using it to cut down trees while their younger partner uses an ax to chop off limbs, dragging the slash to the marsh. When it comes to moving the heavier tree trunks, it is a different matter. Bill tosses Josh the keys to his pickup truck, yelling, "There's rope in the back. Just tie the logs to the bumper and drag them to the marsh. Don't get too close or you'll get stuck in the mud!"

They work the rest of the afternoon at removing trees and brush. Josh panics for a second when he pulls his load a bit too close to the marsh. Quickly detaching the heavy tree trunks from the bumper, he slowly drives out of the bog despite a spinning muddy wheel.

The cutting and hauling work seem to be endless. By 6pm, the thermometer on the side of the camp office still reads nearly ninety-five degrees. In the heat, the 'Three Trees Three' seem to be losing their identity. They appear as constantly moving gray ghosts, absolutely soaked with sweat and covered in dust and ashes.

The smoke becomes heavier. Occasional hot red flames can now be seen in the distance at the bases of towering, dark smoke plumes. There is no question, the fire is slowly moving toward their camp.

By 6pm, the last trees are finally down and slash is moved away from the critical areas. Bill, Josh, and Jose' walk slowly back to the camp office for a rest and to have something to eat and drink.

Once inside, they sit comfortably in canvas chairs in the air-conditioned kitchen. Tired smiles and laughs are the rule when they pull their sweaty, grimy handkerchiefs off their faces. Their ash-covered foreheads are in sharp contrast to their clean cheeks and chins.

Dirty or not, they are hungry and thirsty. Each down a bottle of cold water with a couple of thick bologna sandwiches and a bag of cookies.

Bill sits back. After a relieving belch, he brushes some crumbs off his shirt. "Ahh! That was so good!

"Enjoy your dinner fellows. We'll take a break for another 15 minutes or so, then we have to get back at it."

Jose' and Josh are a little surprised. They thought they were done for the day.

Bill explains, "I've spoken with the Forest Service people again. The situation is bad but it looks OK for us here at Three Trees—for a while. Even though we can already see smoke and flames in the distance they are sure that the fire line won't reach here tonight. Fire fighters will be brought in here by helicopter tomorrow morning and begin setting up a base of operations.

"Our job between now and then is to protect this camp. We have to be especially alert for flying embers in these windy conditions. That job will cost us some sleep. For tonight – and that's for the WHOLE night – we have two very important tasks: watch for embers and keep the office and the tent cabins watered down. I'll give you updates as soon as I get them from the Forest Service."

Jose' and Josh absorb Bill's rapid-fire schedule as quickly as their tired brains will allow. Finally, Jose' holds up both of his hands, "Wait Bill! Wait a minute!" Bill and Josh can hear the exasperation in his voice.

"You are going way too fast. We are all tired as hell! Does your all-night plan take that into consideration?"

Bill answers quietly. "Don't worry, Jose.' Yes, the three of us will get some rest. For sure. But under the circumstances, it won't be for more than a few hours at a time. We'll take turns watering the place down, keeping watch for spot fires, and sleeping.

"Remember, guys, we are volunteers. We didn't sign on for this work. Any one of us can simply say, 'I don't want to do this' and just stay in the air-conditioned office and sleep."

Bill puts his hand on Jose's shoulder and looks him in the eye. "If I heard you right earlier today, Jose', you said, 'Hell, I'll stay.' So, which is it now? Stay and work or get out of town?"

Jose' stands with his hands on his hips. For a moment, he looks down at the toes of his boots— then up at Bill. In a much calmer voice, he says, "Geez, Bill, I'm just really tired. Sorry I went off. Yeah, sure, you can count on me."

Bill pats Jose' on the shoulder. "Thanks. Don't worry about it. We all feel like you do now and then. I think you 'went off' for all of us.

"Now let's see if we can work together to minimize the stress for the night."

"Here's the plan. We'll sleep here in the office. The A/C should help. Take the next 15 minutes or so to move anything else you think you will need over here from your cabin. There's a storage room in the back for you to stash your bags and other personal stuff. You'll be sleeping here on the office floor, so bring your mattresses, sheets, and pillows and blankets—frankly, it's so hot that you probably won't need blankets."

After Josh and Jose' had put their gear in the office, Bill went over his plan. "Think of us as the night watch. Starting in about an hour, each of us will take a 90-minute shift to keep an eye on things. When it's your shift, it's important that you don't just sit around or you'll fall asleep – I guarantee it.

"Your job is to walk around the camp looking for problems— flying embers to be specific. That will keep you focused. Also, while you are out there you will hose down this building, the tent-cabins, and outhouses.

"The generator is running fine, so there will be lots of light around the camp. You'll still need a flashlight so you won't break your leg checking out the dark edges of the area.

Your one rule: If you see anything that is bad — even something that MIGHT be bad – wake us up. And don't forget to wear a wet handkerchief over your nose and mouth when you're outside. That smoke is getting worse."

Jose' and Josh look at each other with weary smiles. Jose' asks Bill, "When do we start?"

Bill looks at his watch. "The sun is behind the highest peaks now. We'll start in 15 minutes, at 8:30pm. First, let's take a walk around the campground together to be sure we all know where the critical areas are."

Josh asks "Who takes first shift?"

Bill pulled a coin out of his pocket and tossed it to Jose.' "I'll take the first shift at 8:30pm, you two flip a coin for the next one."

Josh wins the toss to relieve Bill at 10pm. Jose' follows Josh. They'd each have one more shift before sunrise.

The three of them walk around the camp to set their inspection route before their shifts start. Jose' points to the glow in the canyon to the east and says, matter-of-factly, "Well, here it comes."

Bill looks at the smoke plume illuminated by the blaze. It is definitely brighter and closer. "Yeah, I think we are going to have a hell of a lot of work to do if that thing keeps coming."

Josh can't figure out if he is excited, or worried, or just tired— probably all three. One thing he already knows for sure is that breathing through a wet handkerchief is not fun. It doesn't really keep all of the smoke out.

Back in the office after their tour of the critical areas around the camp, Bill starts his shift while Jose' and Josh drop tiredly onto their mattresses. Josh is asleep almost immediately and Jose' a few minutes later.

After ninety minutes, Bill quietly shakes Josh awake for his first shift. Josh sits up and rubs his eyes. He pulls on his boots and they head for the door as Jose's snores seemed to rattle the office windows. Josh laughs, "I think it's way quieter outside."

Before beginning his inspection of the camp, Bill pats Josh on the shoulder, "Any questions, kid?" Josh shakes his head with a sleepy smile, saying, "I think I've got it down, oh great leader."

Bill repeats his earlier warning, "Remember, if you see anything that you think is weird – that is ANYTHING – come wake us up."

Josh gives a half-hearted salute towards Bill and says, "Aye, Aye, sir."

Tying his wet and, now, very dirty, kerchief over his mouth and nose, he is wide awake as he begins his shift.

The high points of his hour and half tour of the camp are the pulsing glow of the fire in the distance and a few strange noises from the nearby dark woods. His bright flashlight doesn't reveal any forest critters, although he certainly hears them. They sound frightened.

The night goes quickly. When Josh comes back into the office after his last shift, his two co-workers are both awake, drinking coffee. A few minutes later, Jose' steps outside for his final watch.

Bill sits down to relax for a few minutes. He glances up at Josh, "You want to do breakfast? We are having eggs and pancakes. He smiles. "By the way, I've never asked you, can you cook?"

Josh laughs at the idea. "My cooking experience ends with cold cereal and canned fruit. For anything else, I don't think you'd like me to experiment on you and Jose'."

"You are right, my young friend. I would encourage you to fry an egg now and to learn something, but I'd rather not have you practice on me." He laughed, "And I'll bet Jose' feels the same way! Back to KP for you. And keep those dishes clean!"

They chatted a bit longer about the fire and what might happen next. Bill said, "I'll bet we see some Forest Service crews today. That fire is way too close. They need this place as a base and they are going to have to protect it."

Bill began banging around the kitchen, putting breakfast together. It is close to the 5:30 a.m., the end of their shifts. The night skies begin to lighten as the smoky rays of sun begin to spread over the mountain ridges in the east when Jose' steps through the office door after finishing his last shift.

Despite their fractured sleeping schedules, the "Three Trees Three" are feeling good and very hungry. A heavy morning dose of scrambled eggs, fried potatoes, bacon, canned fruit, coffee, Juice, milk, toast and jam disappears quickly.

Leaning back in his chair and looking down at his empty plate, Josh produces a huge belch that resonates across the kitchen. Jose' laughs so hard that he spills his hot coffee in his lap, leading to an even funnier dance and "Ay! Ay! Ow! Ow!" on his way to the sink where he pours a glass of cold water on the problem.

Josh and Bill are nearly rolling on the floor as their uncontrollable laughter ripples around the kitchen, breaking the tension of their situation. A lot of stress has been wiped away by Jose's antics.

Bill pulls out his smart phone and says, "Hey guys, there is a photo-op here. "We can impress our relatives with our dirty faces!" They all dig out their smart-phones and spend a few minutes on the porch of the office with plumes of smoke in the background. "Documenting our smokiness!" as Bill laughingly puts it.

Their relaxed moment is broken abruptly by a very loud, thumping sound. Bill, Jose,' and Josh look up to see a large, twin-bladed helicopter slowly descend out of the smoky morning sky onto the wide landing pad they had prepared the day before. Bill shouts, "Here comes the cavalry!"

21.

The helicopter executes a smooth but noisy landing.

Bill yells, "Hey! It's one of those Sikorsky choppers. With those two big engines, it can haul a lot of people and gear. And we'll see them pull some giant buckets of water out of the lake to dump on hot spots."

His assessment of the load capability is verified as six fire fighters jump out of the craft and begin unloading huge pieces of equipment. Ten minutes later, more noise and whirlwinds of dust are generated by the helicopter as it quickly rises and disappears into the smoky sky.

On the ground, the person obviously in charge waves to the onlookers while she directs her crew to move the unloaded equipment to various points in campground. A few minutes later, she walks over to Bill and his assistants, Josh and Jose' and introduces herself with a smile, "Hi, I'm Ellie Martin, Forest Service. It looks like we'll be your guests for the next couple of days or however long it takes to get this fire under control."

Ellie Martin replaces her flight helmet with a forest service cap and dark glasses. Her short brown ponytail sticks out of the back of the cap. In her mid-thirties, she is obviously in good condition, moving easily around the area to direct her team. She wears a green flight suit with the USFS logo on her shoulder and her name tag over a chest pocket. She is friendly, but there is no doubt who is in charge.

Bill reaches out to shake her hand and introduce himself and Josh and Jose. "Welcome to Three Trees, Ellie. We're here to help.

We managed to give this place a haircut so you could get your helicopters in. Got more for us to do?"

Martin quickly explains the situation. "The fire has spread along a wide front that is approaching from the east. We are not absolutely sure what it's going to do, but we suspect there will be some blow-ups as it moves through a couple of narrow canyons. I don't know if you're familiar with blow-up conditions. That's when hot temperatures and strong winds cause a fire to spread much more rapidly through the crowns of the trees. Although that behavior is more likely to occur several miles from here, east winds will carry embers from those incidents to your front door."

"We expect to see the worst conditions here in 24 to 48 hours. I can't afford to pull enough people off the fire line to expand the safe area you have already cleared. You've done a great job, but there is more to do. I need your help.

Ellie had the full attention of the Three Trees Three. Bill stands with his arms folded, concentrating on her words while thinking about job description for this place that he read before he signed on as manager. It certainly didn't include this activity.

Josh, with his hands in his pockets, was also listening closely. He found himself wondering whether he would rather be here, facing a forest fire, or lost on a side road on his bike, or facing a rattlesnake. He smiles at the thought, and decides that maybe here is better—a little better.

Jose' is thoroughly focused on Ellie's request. The situation is exciting, although the idea of facing down a fire is on the scary side of exciting.

Ellie continues, "I want to be clear. You guys don't have to do anything. You aren't Forest Service personnel." She hesitates. "But If you do decide to help us that will allow me to put three more fire fighters on the line. At this point, that addition is crucial." She paused for a second, looking from face to face, then asks, "What do you want to do?"

Bill looks at Josh and Jose.' They nod to him. He turns to Ellie with the answer of the Three Trees Three, "We're in."

Martin is now very specific in her instructions. She points toward the creek, "We'll use that area to give the choppers a closer spot to fill their water buckets rather than flying ten miles downstream to Mercer's Lake. But we need better – safer – access for the helicopters. On this side of the creek, all trees and brush must be cleared another 10 yards back from that wide section where the water is moving slowly. You guys will do that. We have a couple of chain saws we can give you.

"Our goal is to keep this place as safe as possible for people and equipment. Besides needing room for helicopters to fill their water buckets, other choppers will be in and out of here transporting people and equipment to and from locations near the fire. They must have room to maneuver.

"Do you see the half-dozen or so Jack Pines close to the other side of the creek? You will cut them down close to the ground. You don't have to move them, they just need to be flattened to give the helicopters room to maneuver. Do you understand?

Bill looks at his young assistants. They nod affirmatively. "Yeah, we understand. We can handle it, Ellie. We'll get started as soon as we get our tools together."

Ellie gives them another assignment. "As the fire gets closer, it's important to keep that office building wet. That is now our headquarters and there will be a lot of people inside with the sparks flying outside.

"And keep the surrounding area watered down, especially the tent cabins. We need them to store supplies. If they get dry under this hot sun, the wood and canvas are vulnerable to flying sparks. Obviously, this is a 24-hour-a-day job. If I can find the personnel, I'll give you some extra eyes and hands. In the meantime, you are the ones who have to do it.

"By the way, I have fire suits and masks for all of you." She pointed to one of her assistants. "That's Joe Richards, tell him that I want you guys outfitted in that equipment. He'll give you a quick lesson on its use. Listen carefully! Your life may depend on it."

About 10a.m., Bill, Jose', and Josh carry their fire suits and masks back to their tent cabins. They stop for a few minutes to discuss their quick lesson on the use of the equipment. Jose' says hesitantly, "I THINK I know how these things work. I just hope that we don't have to use them."

Josh agrees with a grunt as he slips the pack of emergency gear over his shoulders. "One more thing to carry around."

A few minutes later, they are back to clearing more brush and trees. Dressed in their protective gear, the sweat runs freely down their shirts as they work in the hot, smokier conditions. They have their smoke masks in their back packs. It's just too hot to put them on.

Jose' stops for a minute and looks around at the changes in the now wide-open campground. "By the time this is over, I think they'll be calling this place 'Camp No Trees!'"

An hour or so later, they notice fire fighters beginning to put on smoke masks. Bill pulls his mask out nods to at Josh and Jose', "We'd better follow their lead. They certainly know more about this than we do."

More helicopters arrive, sometimes two at a time, adding more whirling dust to the smoky air. The differences in appearances of those who had been on the line and their replacements is stark.

Tired, dirty, gray-faced men step out of one helicopter to be replaced by fresh-faced guys in clean outfits. Personnel and equipment are unloaded and loaded in a nearly continuous stream. Other choppers take turns hovering over the creek to refill their huge canvas water buckets to dump on hot spots.

Ellie Martin finishes giving instructions to a group of firefighters about to enter a helicopter and then comes over to talk to Bill, Josh and Jose'. "The bad stuff is just few miles over the hill. Despite the decreasing visibility, the orange glow the distance is good evidence. If you think its busy now, just wait for a half hour. We'll really be hustling!

"Stay out of the way of the firefighters. Their job is to handle the fire, your job is to be safe. At no time should you approach a burning area. Keep those smoke masks and your gloves on and be sure your **fire suit** is in its pack on your back."

Pointing to one of her crew, she says, "Ask that guy for **fire shelters**. He'll give you a briefing on their use and you'll do a quick practice getting into your shelters. Be safe." She turns and walks rapidly toward an arriving helicopter to speak to the crew.

Bill, Jose, and Josh receive brief instructions and go through a sweaty practice session getting into their protective gear. They listen carefully to the fire fighter's warning, "Don't forget your gloves and be quick!" Then he was gone.

A little later, they make their way to the kitchen where there is plenty of work to do. The place is jammed with ash-covered firefighters coming and going. They are pleased to see that a load of rations has more than doubled their food supply.

Things don't change much the next few hours. Helicopters shuttle firefighters, water buckets, and other equipment back and forth from the camp to the fire front. Ellie Martin flies on to another problem area to direct operations there.

Back at the campground, it is apparent that the dry east winds have decreased a bit. Unfortunately, that change doesn't seem to have much impact on the forest fire. Visibility is still bad and the ever-present smoke is a hazy black and white mix with sporadic injections of orange flames.

After lunch, there is a break in the long line of hungry and thirsty firefighters. Bill stands on the steps of the camp office and asks no one in particular, "I wonder what's next?"

Josh answers as he steps out on the porch. "For me, I had better call home. If my folks have heard about this fire, they'll be worried. They know I'm in the area. By the way, if either of you guys want to use my smart phone to call anybody, just let me know."

Josh goes into back into the office where he had thrown his bags and pulls out his phone. He sits on his sleeping bag to make his call. His dad answers. He is very concerned. "Josh, where are you? We have seen pictures of that fire up your way. From the maps and reports, it looks like it is close to where you are."

Josh was quick to play down any danger. "You're right, Dad, there is a big fire in the mountains east of here, but it's miles away. About the only effects it has had on us is that all the recreational campers have gone and it's a bit smoky. I'm inside our camp office now—no smoke problem in here. The place is air conditioned, so it's cool, too. And when we do go outside, we have smoke masks to wear, courtesy of the Forest Service."

Bob Mayer, breathes a sigh of relief at his son's description. "With all the firefighters up there, I suppose that there isn't much for you to do except to watch and stay out of the way."

Josh hesitates to correct his dad, but he finally says, "I wish that was true. Even though the fire is miles away, we have been working our tails off. Three Trees is now a sort of base camp for operations up at the fire line. The three of us who usually man the camp have been busy cutting and moving slash and watering down the buildings. It's nothing like the tough job those people have on the fire line, but we definitely haven't been sitting around.

"Don't worry, Dad. We are not on the fire line and you can bet we'll be out of here fast if there is a problem. Other than the slash removal, my buddies and I are mainly making sure the camp is in good shape for the firefighters to use as a base of operations. We have lots of work and long hours, but nothing dangerous." While he speaks to his father, Josh looks through the window at a Forest Service crew moving purposefully around the smoky environment of the campground. He hopes his words to his dad are right.

Josh persists with his positive tone and a chuckle, "Dad! I told you not to worry. I'm chopping wood – I'm not fighting any fires!"

Bob asks a few more questions and gives the phone to his wife, Lynn. Her concern is evident in her voice, "Now Josh, you stay out of trouble. Be safe and call again …soon!"

Josh can hear the worry in her voice. He tells her that he is in no danger and promises to stay in touch, adding, "Mom, be sure to remind Dad that I'm working on a very busy project up here. I may not be able to call and, if I do, it'll be late. I'm in good hands with all these firefighters around. It's exciting and interesting. I'm learning a lot. That's for sure."

Now Kelly. For some weird internet reason, his connection to her fails. He finally manages to send a short text.

KELLY PHONE NOT WORKING NOW WILL TRY LATER MISS YOU MUCH LOVE JOSH

22.

T he next morning brings a favorable wind shift with much better visibility and cooler temperatures. A few columns of smoke are still visible to the east, a sign of the persistence of the fire. Otherwise, the air is surprisingly fresh at Three Trees.

Despite the improvement, the campground is still busy. The Large helicopters drop in at regular intervals to collect buckets of water from the creek while smaller helicopters pick up and drop off personnel and equipment at the, now, much wider parking lot near the camp store.

Even though Bill and his two assistants have washed up and put on clean blue camp aprons for the breakfast shift in the kitchen, their faces still have a gray and dusty resemblance to the firefighters and helicopter crews they are feeding. That appearance might be the same in as past mornings, but attitudes are very much different. Easy laughter punctuates relaxed conversations. There is a sense that they are near the end of a tough job.

When breakfast is over and the crowd of hungry firefighters returns to their tasks, Josh gives a tired smile to Jose', saying "I think we're about done. If I never see an axe, a shovel, a water bucket, a fire hose or …" he yawned "… or a kitchen ever again, it will be too soon."

Jose' rubs his dusty face and stifles his own yawn as he agrees with his friends. "I think I need a normal job—you know, eight hours a day, someone else feeding me, no smoke, and no ashes in my teeth!"

Josh suddenly slaps his hands together, "Hey, Jose, how's this for an idea? How about we take some pictures on our phones to impress our relatives and friends with our dirty faces?" Jose likes the idea and they walk back to the camp office to find Bill and to get one of the Forest Service guys to take a picture of the three of them.

When they see the results, there's a lot of laughing. Bill shakes his head in amazement, "This is bizarre! We look like space aliens. Nobody we know will recognize us. Send me copies of these. They are keepers!"

They are soon back at work, cleaning up the kitchen while continuing to come down from the stresses of the last few days. Bill and his two assistants are having a relaxed conversation about the future, especially about what's next for the Camp Three Trees.

Bill knows. "From a few conversations I've had with Ellie and some others in the fire crew, it looks like Three Trees will now be run by Forest Service personnel, year-round. We've had some very dry winters with a record number of fires in the Sierra in the past few summers. They don't expect things to change in the next year or so. They will continue to use Three Trees as a summer campground, but they'll also turn it into a fully equipped fire suppression unit. I'm not clear on the details, but I've heard Ellie and her crew talking about these changes more than once. I suspect that this will be the last time Three Trees will be run by guys like us."

Bill had to raise his voice to be heard over the noise of another helicopter bringing in fire fighters and their gear. With its blades continuing to turn, it is quickly unloaded. The ground crew quickly moves away from the departing chopper and its dust cloud.

The engine noise is suddenly doubled as another larger helicopter arrives to scoop up a huge bucket of water from the nearby creek.

Suddenly, an extremely loud, grinding collision between the two helicopters causes everyone on the ground to dive for cover under vehicles and behind buildings. They look back to see the larger helicopter spinning wildly out of control then hitting the ground on its side with a thunderous impact. Pieces of rotor blades, torn metal, and Plexiglas rain across the campground.

A moment later, the second, smaller helicopter smashes into the base of a tree a hundred yards away. It comes to a rest leaning at a steep angle on a broken landing gear.

Hatches of the large chopper burst open at the first crash site. Five men come tumbling out, some hobbling. The ground crew rushes over to help them move quickly away from the twisted remains of the chopper. Fortunately, there is only smoke—no fire despite the noticeable odor of spilled fuel. Someone yells, "Is that everybody?"

The pilot, the last man out, waves his arms and shouts, "We're all out!"

A crew of firefighters quickly begin hosing the down the crash area and pumping fire retardant onto the hot engine. Bill, Josh, and Jose' stand well back from the scene, watching. They are riveted by the quick reactions of the fire fighters helping injured crew members and controlling the fire in the mangled, smoking helicopter.

More firefighters run to the other crash site to help the crew get out. Suddenly, that crash site is rattled by a muffled explosion followed by an outbreak of flames in the tail section. The fire causes the rescuers to hesitate for a moment. Then they cautiously move closer. The two crew members inside the helicopter make no visible effort to get out. With heavy smoke pouring out of the engine, four firefighters push close enough to reach through the smoke and bang on the jammed hatch in an attempt to open it. There are no reactions from the two men in the cockpit. Flames spread rapidly around the wreckage.

One of the rescuers yells, "They are twisted up in there. I think they're dead. We can't get past that fire anyway. Too much fuel on board. Better get back before it blows!"

Two of the crew manning hoses moves away while keeping water streaming onto the burning ship. Others run off to work on keeping the fire from spreading into the forest.

From his safe vantage point, Josh's attention is focused on the activity around the smaller helicopter. He suddenly grabs Bill by the arm. "Bill, I saw somebody move their hand." He turns around and shouts to one of the nearby firefighters. "There's still someone alive in there!"

One of the firemen yelled, "It's too late! With all that fuel, it's going to explode! Get back!"

Before anyone could stop him, Josh runs to the side of the helicopter, dodging flames, then using his shovel to pry open the badly bent hatch. He isn't prepared for the heat. He has left his gloves and mask back in the office. His jeans are smoking. Fire licks at his unprotected face and hands. He can smell singed hair.

Putting all of his weight on his shovel, the hatch finally bursts open with a loud, metallic crack. Josh quickly climbs in and pulls the harness off one of the pilots, yelling at him to get out. The man is unresponsive. Josh hauls him out of his seat and drags the limp body to Jose' and Bill who are also dodging flames as they step over the broken hatch cover at their feet to get close to the crashed ship. They quickly move the injured crew member away, yelling back at Josh to get out.

Instead, Josh goes back inside the helicopter to get the other pilot. Smoke and fire are rapidly enveloping the crashed ship. Josh's breathing becomes more ragged; his mouth and nose are burning from the acrid smoke. He's coughing. Wiping smoke and grit particles out of his eyes, his skin feels slick, like jelly. He yells at himself, "C'mon, just grab the guy and run! Get out of this oven!"

He reaches around the flames now coming up through a hole in the floor and unbuckles the second pilot, and pulls him quickly out of his seat. The pilot's eyes are open. One of his arms is twisted at a strange angle—clearly badly broken. For a moment, Josh can't take his eyes off of the pilot's other arm. It looks like a piece of charred wood.

Straining to exit the helicopter, Josh yells at the grimacing, injured man, "Hang on, you're almost out!"

Suddenly dizzy, Josh shakes his head to clear his dimming vision as he drags the injured man to the hatch. With his last bit of energy, he strains to lower the pilot into the arms of Bill and Jose.' A strange darkness begins to close around him. The last thing he remembers is Jose' yelling, "C'mon Josh! Get out of there!"

23.

J osh opens his eyes. He shakes his head. Where is he? He looks around. A nurse dressed in blue scrubs stands next to him with her fingers on his wrist, checking his pulse. His buddies, Jose' and Bill, stand at the foot of the bed watching him.

Josh begins to speak, but his voice sounds muffled. He tries to touch for his face. He realizes that his hands are wrapped in gauze and he is wearing a mask attached to a long tube.

The nurse speaks quietly to him, "Joshua Mayer, you are in the Byron City Hospital. Take it easy, you are on the mend. Your buddies are here to see how you are doing."

Bill and Jose' had to stifle a laugh when Josh mumbles his first words, "I think I'm in a bag!"

His nurse smiles, "It's not quite a bag, but it is something that you will have to get used to for a couple of days. You'll be drinking through a straw."

She showed him how to manage a sip of water.

"And, another thing, you won't be getting up to pee. If you have to go, just go. You are all hooked up with our plumbing—something called a catheter."

Josh moves his bandaged hand over his crotch to feel the catheter tube, following the line down to the yellow bag on the side of the bed.

"Otherwise I've got a little bad news and mostly good news for you, young fella.

"The bad news is that, for the moment, you are going to be a little uncomfortable. You've had burns over exposed areas of your upper body, particularly your face, hands, and arms. We are giving you some meds to reduce the pain. That mask will give you some extra oxygen for a while. For now, just relax and rest."

The good news is that you are alive and healing. You will get better, much better.

The nurse expertly takes his vital signs as she continued speaking to him. "By the way, we could not find identification on you. How old are you?"

He gives a muffled response, "Eighteen."

She rolls her eyes, "Right, and I am Captain America. Well, I'm not going to worry about that right now. Your medical bill is being taken care of by the Forest Service. I'm sure they will check your number of birthdays before you get out of here."

"Your friends here have been briefed on your situation. They can stay here for another five or ten minutes, then come visit tomorrow."

The nurse left Josh in the company of Bill and Jose.' Bill stood at the foot of the bed, cowboy hat in hand. He looked down at his well-wrapped friend, a worried smile on his face. "Josh, you nut! You almost killed yourself! "Geez, you had us worried.

"You're lucky you don't have worse burns. The pilots from one of those crashed helicopters are down the hall. They both have severe burns and broken bones—lucky to be alive.

"Can you understand me?"

A hoarse and slightly muffled, "Yeah" came through the bandages on Josh's face.

Jose' leans close to his friend, "Hey man, you almost became a torch out there. I was glad to hear the nurse say what she did. After a little healing, it looks like you're going to be Ok." He stifles a chuckle, "Except for that amazing sunburn. Man, you are red!"

Josh whispers a question. Bill has to put his ear closer. Josh repeats, "Did the nurse say the two pilots in the helicopter got out?"

Bill nods with a smile. "They got out, thanks to you, Josh. Both of them are in this hospital with some nasty burns and some fractures. healing will take some time, but they'll be okay."

What he didn't say was that it was a very close call. Those pilots are lucky to be alive.

As Josh's mind clears, he begins to wonder what to tell his parents and Kelly. And when? Certainly, he has to call home soon. The fire and the crashes will probably make the news back there. He asks Jose' to bring his smart phone in when he visits next time.

Jose' pulls Josh's phone out of his pocket. "I'm way ahead of you on that one, amigo. Here it is!"

Wrestling with his awkward bandages and painful fingers, Josh attempts to send text messages to Kelly and to his mom and dad. He can't do it—too awkward. He looks over at Jose.' "I'm not doing too well with this thing. My fingers are a little too fat. Can I dictate a message to you to send to my folks?"

"Absolutely, Josh! Let me have that thing and dictate away!"

This is for my family. Josh cleared his throat and spoke slowly, "THE FIRE IS OUT. USFS FIRE FIGHTERS DID A GREAT JOB. ALL OK. CLEANING UP NOW. CAMPERS HAVE ALL GONE BCUZ OF FIRE. WILL BE HOME IN ABOUT A WEEK. WILL SEND YOU EXACT SCHED SOON. JOSH"

Jose' winces at the text message. "What is this 'ALL OK' stuff? You are sitting – lying – in a hospital, wrapped from head to foot, can't really move, and peeing in a bag. Your text doesn't quite capture on the real situation, Josh. Do you really want me to send it?"

Josh nods his bandaged head with hoarse, "Please Jose,' just send it. I'll be OK by the time I get home. All they would do is worry. Geez, if they knew the whole story, they'd probably jump in their car and drive up here. I'm going to be alright and I can tell them all about it when I get home ... please send it.

"OK, my man, your message is on its way.

Writing Kelly is not easy. Josh doesn't think he should use the words he really wants to, like "MISS YOU" and "LOVE.". He ends up with: HEY KELLY. COMING HOME EARLY. CAN'T WAIT TO SEE YOU!! WILL SEND MORE INFO LATER. JOSH

Jose' grins at Josh's second text message. "'Can't wait to see you.' Hmm. Sounds like love to me." He laughed. Josh's burns hid his blush. "C'mon Jose', she's just a friend."

Jose' laughs. "Oh, sorry, just a friend, huh?" Will I meet her some day?"

24.

Two days later, Josh Is released from the hospital to return to Three Trees Campground. His bandages are mostly gone and He trims his singed eyebrows and a few patches of scorched hair on one side of his head then leans close to the mirror in the wash room to check out the damage. Except for a couple of burn spots on his forehead and his hands, he looks like he has had had a long day in the sun.

Forest Service personnel take over Three Trees to provide security for the wreckage of the two crashed helicopters and clean-up of the camp and surrounding burned area.

Bill, Jose', and Josh prepare to leave. They all have a good laugh when Josh pulls his dusty bike from under the cabin. Holding onto the seat and the handlebars he leans the bike away from him and gives it his first visual inspection in what seems like months. The fire hadn't touched it, but the tires were flat and the frame was coated in ash. "Damn, riding this thing only a few weeks ago seems like ancient history now."

Bill says, "I don't think you'll be going anywhere on those wheels for a while!"

Josh replies, "Nah, it's OK. The rear wheel hub still needs a bit of repair. With that, a little cleaning up, and some air in the tires, it'll be good to go."

Patting the bike seat, he smiled happily. "There are still a lot more miles in it."

Jose' laughs at Josh, pointing at his bike, "Somebody told me once that you have to be a little crazy to be a cyclist. I think you and your machine have proved that."

Two days later, Josh is standing on the roadside waiting for his bus home when Bill and Jose' walk up to say goodbye. Josh is ready for the trip with his two saddle bags and sleeping bag bundled alongside his disassembled bike.

Bill shakes Josh's hand, "Other than looking like you have had a helluva long day in the sun, I think the time here has agreed with you. And, if I'm not mistaken, I'd say you've put on some muscle." He laughs, "You're not quite that skinny kid who rode his bike up to the gate **five weeks** ago."

Jose' agrees, slapping Josh on his shoulder, "You've grown up, boy!"

Josh looks down, a little embarrassed over his friends' attention. Feeling his face get warm, he realizes that it was a good thing he has his "sunburn" – nobody can tell he is doing that stupid blushing!

Becoming more serious, Josh asks, "Where are you going from here, Jose'? Any ideas for your future?"

"Mmm, not completely sure. "He looks thoughtfully up at the Ponderosa Pines that shaded them. "To tell the truth, I think I'd like to work for the Forest Service."

He glanced at Bill, explaining. "Our boss over there thinks that, on the basis of my work record—especially this summer, I should be able to get some related work. He showed me some links to USFS jobs.

"In the long run, I need to go back to school; to Junior College, maybe more. It won't be easy. I wasn't the best student in high school and I have been out and away from the books for a year." He stretches his arms above his head, "What I feel good about is that, for the first time in my life, I have a plan for the future." He smiled, "Work to do! I'm ready!"

"How about you, Josh?"

"Well, I have to finish high school. As you guys have probably figured out, I have been bullshitting everybody in camp about my age. I'm only 16. I'll be a junior this year – two years to go. I'm not sure what I want to do."

Josh looks over Jose's shoulder for a second, taking in the forest and mountains that stretched into the distance. "I'm a bit like you, Jose.' Our summer in this place has turned me on to forestry. I like the outdoors, I like the people; I like what the Forest Service does. Maybe we'll see each other wandering through the woods someday, dressed in USFS uniforms—telling the bears what to do—and I'll probably be working for you!"

They both have a good laugh. Jose' slaps his hands together, "And we'll probably be working for Bill! Oh no! The Camp Three Trees boys together again – wouldn't that be something!"

Just as the words come out of Jose's mouth, Bill walks up. "What are you two misfits laughing at?"

"Josh and Jose' look at each other then back at Bill, cracking up again. Jose bowed too his boss, "At you, Mr. Bill! At you, oh great leader!"

Bill shakes his head saying, "At least, today, I'm going to get rid of one of you crazies!"

Josh becomes a little more serious, "Bill, what do you plan to do when both of us have left?

He crosses his arms and looks up at the blue sky. He was silent for a few seconds. Then he looks back at Jose' and Josh. "Good question. I'm not sure, either. My work has evidently gotten the attention of some higher-ups. Rumor has it that there might even be some sort of new job for me in the works. In the meantime, Jose' and I will be cleaning up around here."

He grins, "It'll be tough without you to push around, Josh!"

They have a good laugh, then Josh becomes a bit more serious. "Bill, I want to thank you and Jose' for everything you have done for me, from teaching me how to clean outhouses to pulling my butt out of that fire. It has been a hell of a summer, I'll never forget it –"

He chuckles, "But I might forget you guys!

"Nah, I'm kidding. Your mugs are stuck in my gray matter until forever!"

The bus arrives, kicking up a cloud of dust as it stops in front of Josh and his friends. With handshakes and shoulder bumps around, Josh, his bags, and his bike are on the bus and on their way home.

25.

Josh unloads his luggage at the bus terminal in Argyle as Bob Mayer stands quietly in the crowd nearby, watching his son. He can't help but notice the changes that have taken place over the summer. Josh seems taller, definitely with more muscle, and broader in the shoulders. His blonde hair was not really long but then, not really short. Kind of a crooked, shaggy cut. Bob smiles at the thought that perhaps his son is his own barber. He notices Josh's sunburned face, likely a reflection of some long hours of outdoor work.

Bob finally walks up to Josh, "Hey son, great to see you! Let me carry your stuff. Your mom will be along in a minute."

Josh reaches his hand out to shake his dad's hand, then laughing, they give each other bear hugs.

Stepping back to hold his son at arm's length, Bob smiles, saying, "Josh, you look good! It looks like your ride and that camp job really agreed with you!"

Josh nods with a broad smile. "You're right, Dad. It was hard, but really interesting work. Good people. I can't believe how lucky I was to step off my bike and into such a great job.

"My boss and the guy I worked with were super. We got along fine and, wow! Did we do a lot! If my legs were in shape from the riding, the rest of me got into shape digging ditches and chopping wood and hauling it around." He rubs his happy face, unsuccessfully stifling a yawn, "It still makes me tired just to think about!"

Bob is not only pleased to see his son safe, sound, and in good shape, but he also has the distinct impression he is a more confident and happier young man. "Joshua, what about that fire? From everything I saw and heard, it was very close to Three Trees."

"Not a big problem, Dad. The fire was actually several miles east of us. We were just a very busy support base for the fire fighters. My main jobs were feeding them and washing dishes."

Josh asks, "Where's Mom?"

"Across the street at the grocery store, she'll be back in a few minutes. You can expect a great homecoming dinner this evening.

"By the way, Ed sends a big 'Hi!' He's settled in his new university, already busy finding out that college is a bit more demanding than high school."

Josh listens carefully to his dad's update on the beginning his brother's university adventure out in Colorado. "Looks like he'll be majoring in business, following me," he smiles. It's an exciting time for him."

Bob is a multitasking parent, busy talking about his older son's introduction to college life and absorbing his youngest son's summer adventure. He puts his hand on Josh's shoulder. "By the way, son, Ed heard about the fire near Three Trees. He's asked several times about you. When we get home, you should email or text him. Adding, "Joshua, I know you and Ed have often been at odds, but I also know that those issues will pass as you get older. The main thing now is to stay in touch."

"Sure, I'll let him know that I'm back." Josh grinned, "Safe and sound in the arms of the family!

"And Dad, speaking of college, this summer, I have had a lot of discussions with my friends and some Forest Service folks about working for them later on. No details yet. I just thought you'd be glad to hear that I'm starting to think about a forestry major when I go to college."

Ed is pleasantly surprised at Josh's ideas about life after high school. He begins to realize that, perhaps he hasn't given him enough breathing room when Ed was around. He reaches over and pats Josh's arm, "That's great news, son! Be sure and tell your mom."

He's happy at the thought of sitting with his mother and telling her about his adventures. "I promise to give her the whole story, Dad."

Josh looks forward to hugging his mom, although it isn't really family that is filling his thoughts. It is Kelly. He feels that he's almost crazy not having seen her for so long. He had texted her telling her when he would arrive. But looking around, she is nowhere to be seen.

He unpacks his bicycle expertly and quickly: attaches the wheels on; pumps the tires; piles his gear on the rack, and rolls it to the car. His dad tosses him the keys to the trunk. While Josh loads his equipment, his father continues to pepper him with questions about his ride and his work at Three Trees.

"Josh, you have not only beefed up, but that awful acne has disappeared, it does look like you got a heck of a sunburn!" Although Josh is a bit embarrassed by his dad's observations, he is pleased, too. It had been a good, exciting summer. He told his dad that he had even saved a few dollars.

While they continue their conversation, Lynn quietly walks up behind them. She listens and watches her husband and son interact for several minutes. Josh's animated descriptions of his adventures at the campground cause tears to fill her eyes with the realization that her youngest son has changed quickly over the short summer. His look and his attitude are so positive—*my little one has grown up – so fast.*

Her, "Hi Josh," interrupts the father-son conversation. She kisses Josh's cheek. They hug, then she pushes him out to arm's length, saying, "My goodness, Josh, you have a heck of a sunburn! And who gave you that haircut? She laughs, "It's a bit crooked and your eyebrows look like they have been trimmed by a hedge cutter. Why would you trim your eyebrows?"

Josh hugged her, "Hey Mom! It's so great to see you. About my hair. It got shaggy after a few weeks and there was no barber for miles. So, I to cut it myself." He shrugs his shoulders. "I'm just not a very good barber … especially in the woods, with dull scissors and a hand mirror!"

She smiles at his somewhat odd explanation and gives a sigh of relief saying, "We're sure glad you're finally home! From what I heard you telling your dad, you had a wonderful time.

"By the way, Josh, your brother is off to college. He is a busy guy now with classes and all."

"Dad told me. Ed and I will be texting, for sure!"

Josh is distracted from their conversation. He looks over his mother's shoulder to see a familiar figure. It is Kelly, standing across the street in a swarm of passengers rushing in and out of the bus terminal. She watches as Josh's parents hover around him.

He begins to walk toward her, shouting over his shoulder, "Mom and Dad, I see someone I know. Give me a second." Then he runs.

His parents watch him go. They are surprised when a pretty, red-haired girl breaks away from the crowd and runs to him. Josh and Kelly stop, facing each other. They reach out and touch hands. Josh wants to kiss her and Kelly wanted to kiss him, but they are a little embarrassed with Josh's family hovering nearby. Finally, Josh leans over and whispers in her ear, "I really missed you, Kelly."

He can't stop looking at her face framed in red curls, her beautiful blue eyes, and her wonderful smile. "Kelly, you are so – so beautiful!"

She blushes, holding tightly to his hands. She begins to notice how much Josh has changed. He is more muscular and taller. He speaks in his same soft tones, but with a certainty that she hadn't noticed before.

She gently touches one hand to his face. "You let yourself get sunburned and you got yourself a funny haircut," she laughed.

A few minutes later, Josh and Kelly walk hand-in-hand to where his parents are standing.

"Mom and Dad, I want you to meet a very good friend. This is Kelly Flynn."

Lynn is nearly in tears realizing the sweet connection between Josh and Kelly. She reaches out to give Kelly a warm handshake. And Bob can't help but notice the sweet infatuation of these young people. He is speechless for a few seconds, but he recovers enough to say a smiling, warm "Hello, Kelly."

A few moments later, she is invited to Josh's homecoming dinner. "Come home with us now," his mother urged. "Certainly, you two have more to talk about."

Kelly looks at Josh who is nodding. "It's OK, Kelly. C'mon home with us, you can call your parents from our place."

26.

The week leading up to the new semester is so jammed that Josh hardly has time to think about his exciting summer. Now he has to get ready for school and reclaim his old jobs.

He is glad to discover that, although most of his replacements for his gardening jobs have been good, his customers are all happy to have him back. And Mr. Steeler is particularly pleased when Josh returns to that job. He invites Josh to sit and chat for a while, asking about his summer and telling him about developments at the store. There is some good news.

"Josh, I know you have only been here for 15 minutes or so, but I'm afraid that you're already behind in your work!" He chuckles. "I'm kidding … but, in a way it's true. My son has had to get back to college a little sooner than we had originally planned and I've gotten very busy. I need you now for at least 15 hours-a-week, more if you can handle it. Are you up for it?"

Josh doesn't hesitate, "Yes sir, I'll do it!"

Another exciting development is an offer of better pay. Josh quickly figures that he can find the time for work at Steeler's if he cuts back on his gardening jobs. He'll offer his best summer replacements a chance to keep their customers permanently.

At home, with his brother away to college in Colorado, Josh finds himself the focus of his parents. Bob and Lynn can't seem to hear enough about "Josh's summer adventure," as his dad put it. Mealtime is filled with Josh's descriptions of his bike ride and his work at Three Trees. Bob and Lynn often find themselves shaking their heads in wonder at his stories. Josh is careful to stay away from his hospital stay and its causes. He isn't really sure what he can say about that without worrying his parents.

One evening just before school is scheduled to start, Bob sits in the living room reading a recent News Magazine. It carried a detailed report about the fire in the mountains near Three Trees. Bob is fascinated by the story and the aerial photos showing the footprint of the fire – 1000's of acres of blackened mountain slopes. The location of Three Trees Campground is clearly indicated on a map of the area.

The article describes the efforts of the fire fighters to get the fire under control, then briefly mentions the collision of the two helicopters, ironically, as conditions were actually improving. There isn't much detail except one brief statement about "— heroic efforts by ground personnel to rescue of two pilots from a burning helicopter."

When his wife walks in, he looks up, saying, "Lynn, I think Josh was right. That was quite an exciting summer at Three Trees. You ought to read this report."

A few days later, Josh reconnects with his buddy, Ron. His friend's summer was tough for a few weeks as the family dealt with his mom's illness. He took over fixing meals and caring for his little brother and sister while his Dad spent long hours between his business and the hospital. Ron worked hard to keep the kids positive about his Mom's recovery. She spent two weeks in the hospital. Now, **six** weeks later, she is up and around, getting better every day.

The first time Ron and Josh see each other after the long summer, they are happy guys, bumping shoulders and giving each other high-fives. Josh tells about his trip with Ron pressing him for many details. They immediately begin making plans to start biking again on the weekends, as soon as Josh can get his bike fixed. And they are already talking about a trip for next summer.

Even before school starts, Kelly and Josh find a few moments to return to their favorite place on campus, 'Their tree.' Some leaves are already starting to yellow and fall in the heat of the late summer. Dry walnuts crunch under their feet.

Both of them are working and they know that their activities will increase even more with classes and plenty of homework in the semester ahead. Their brief meetings give them a little break to say 'hi!' and laugh about life, and hold hands for a few minutes.

The first school assembly of the year is held the Friday before classes began. As usual, the Westward High School auditorium is filled with students, teachers, and administrators. Usually there is only a scattering of parents at these assemblies but today is different. For some reason, parents and many others fill the seats behind the students. In fact, Josh is surprised to see that his parents are there.

Bob leans over to speak to his wife. He has to raise his voice so he can be heard above the noise of the crowd. "Lynn, tell me one more time why we are here. I can't remember coming to any school assemblies since Ed and Josh were freshmen."

She answers with a shrug, "I'm not exactly sure myself. Something to do with Josh and his class, or … frankly, the person who called us and encouraged us to come wasn't very clear. Maybe our son has been selected to be on the student council? Wouldn't that be a nice surprise to start his Junior Year? I guess we'll just have to wait." She pats her husband's arm, smiling in anticipation. "This is kind of exciting, isn't it, Bob?"

He smiled, "Ah, kids. They make us a little crazier every year."

The school Principal, John Owens, rises from his seat and walks purposefully to the lectern to give a warm welcome to all. He begins his presentation with the usual summary of the previous year's accomplishments in academics and extracurricular activities followed by a bright forecast for the coming year. The crowd is appreciative and shows their support with warm applause and some cheers, especially in anticipation of the upcoming football season.

Near the end of the program, conversations among the restless students rise in volume. Principal Owens holds his hands up, asking for quiet. "I have one more, very important item.

"This past summer, one of our students accomplished an important and unselfish act that I would like to recognize. Before I do, I will ask for some help."

At Owens' signal, three individuals move quietly up the aisle from the back of the auditorium. They wear U.S. Forest Service patches on the shoulders of their **tan and green uniforms**. Josh blinks a couple of times, not quite believing what he sees. The person leading the group is Ellie Martin, the USFS fire boss at Three Trees.

Two of the group, dressed in civilian clothes are, yes — Bill Lyndon and Jose' Serrano! On the stage, they are joined by two other Forest Service employees, one on crutches and another in a wheelchair with one arm in a cast.

Ellie approaches the podium. "Ladies and Gentlemen, I'm Ellie Martin of the U.S. Forest Service. I apologize for what may seem an unusual group to attend your high school gathering; however, we are here on a mission.

"That mission is to recognize one of your own who, only a few weeks ago, displayed heroic behavior critical in a rescue effort after the crash of two of our helicopters." While she speaks, Ellie's eyes search the audience until they finally rest on Josh.

"The helicopters had been fighting a large and extremely dangerous forest fire in the Northern Sierra Nevada. Their base camp was a place called Camp Three Trees where landing pads had recently been created to allow two of our helicopters to shuttle in and out with firefighters and equipment. Unfortunately, on this day, just as the fire was being brought under control, these two aircraft collided over Three Trees and crashed."

The audience is absolutely silent, their attention riveted on Ellie as she describes the accident. "The crew of one helicopter was able to get out of their aircraft and run for safety. That wasn't the case with the second chopper. The two pilots were injured seriously and were trapped inside. Without any concern for his own safety, your fellow student, Josh Mayer, a summer employee at Camp Three Trees, broke into the burning ship and pulled the unconscious pilots out of the cockpit and into the hands his two fellow workers, Bill Lyndon and Jose' Serrano."

She turns and motions to Bill and Jose' to come forward. A long and loud applause greets them.

Ellie pauses for a few seconds to let the audience absorb her description of the rescue. "These two men were critical in carrying the injured pilots to safety and in rescuing Josh who had collapsed at the door of the burning helicopter."

Josh Mayer suffered burns and smoke inhalation to the extent that he spent three days in the hospital. By all indications, he has healed well. "Josh, please come up here so everyone can see what a hero looks like."

Josh hesitates, having a hard time believing what he is hearing. He leans over to one of his classmates and whispers, "Did they say my name?"

Slapping him on the shoulder, his buddy announces loudly, "Hey, Josh. You're the man! Get up there!"

Josh approaches the stage in the midst of thunderous applause and cheers from the now-standing audience. He steps up next to Bill and Jose' and reaches across to shake their hands. He looks back at the ocean of faces in the audience, hoping he can see Kelly. No, just too many people. He gives an embarrassed wave to the noisy throng.

Ellie invites the two pilots to come forward. One hobbles up on his crutches while the other wheels himself up to the microphone. The man in the wheelchair takes the mic to say, "Neither of us is a speaker, so we flipped a coin. I lost," he laughs.

Then, turning very serious, he points to Bill, Jose', and Josh. "Without a doubt, these three guys saved our lives. We'll never forget them." With more applause ringing in their ears, the two pilots move to the back of the stage where they shake hands with Jose', Bill, and Josh.

Ellie looks across the assembly room. "I want to close our presentation with a picture that catches the wonderful attitude of these three men in the face of a disastrous forest fire. Something that all of you high school students – all of us – can take away from this ceremony."

She nods to the projectionist. A screen is lowered at the back of the stage. Almost immediately, a large picture appears of three men standing in very smoky conditions. They are somewhat ghostly with gray and dusty clothes, faces, and hair – Bill, Jose', and Josh – laughing and giving the 'V for victory' sign.

She explained, "This photo was taken on the last tough fire day, just before the crashes. For a long week, with little sleep and frequent disregard for their own safety, these three gave their best when the situation was the worst. They spent night hours scouting for flying embers and long days cutting trees and brush and moving the slash away from the critical helicopter staging area.

"I want to emphasize again that they are not Forest Service employees. At the time, they were employees at a small campground that we took over as a staging base to fight the fire. They didn't have to stay. But they did – and they worked shoulder-to-shoulder with our crews. And, the amazing thing is that, without any hesitation, they came through at that critical instant when the two helicopters collided and crashed. They did what was needed without regard for their own safety. If I ever saw heroes, these guys are heroes. We thank them and honor them today."

Smiling broadly, she motioned for Bill, Jose', and Josh to come forward, with a laugh, "Now they stand before you – with clean faces!"

Josh's parents are speechless. Never in their thoughts about who Josh is or what he would become, had they imagined him a hero – standing up to fire – saving lives. His mom is soon in tears and even his dad is choked up. From her seat a few rows away, Kelly is crying and cheering for this boy she loves.

The audience stands with a long and sincere applause for Josh and his buddies. They did it together.

End

www.ingramcontent.com/pod-product-compliance
Lightning Source LLC
Chambersburg PA
CBHW051209120626
46547CB00013B/1265